Street, Buenos Aires

Endpaper:
Tiles, Barcelona

Cover:
River, Prague

THE NOSTALGIC HEART

Text and images © 2006 by David Coggins

All rights reserved
Published in 2006 by Cobalt Press
Printed in Canada

ISBN-10: 0-9788225-0-1
ISBN-13: 978-0-9788225-0-7

Designed by Kristen McDougall

www.cobaltpress.com

THE NOSTALGIC HEART

DAVID COGGINS

Cobalt Press
Minneapolis
2006

Lantern, Kyoto

To Wendy, David, and Sarah

Chandni Chowk, Delhi

There is nothing more exciting to me than arriving in a new city. . . . Eventually — and the longer it takes, the more comfortable I feel — one reaches a crowded old centre, the nostalgic heart. . . .

PAUL RAMBALI
The Cities and Jungles of Brazil

Market, Salvador, Bahia

CONTENTS

PREFACE		12
THE OTHER AMERICA	MINNEAPOLIS	17
	LIMA	18
	CUZCO	28
	QUITO	37
	SANTIAGO	48
	BUENOS AIRES	64
	RIO DE JANEIRO	79
	SALVADOR, BAHIA	86
THE END OF RESTLESSNESS	BARCELONA	100
	PRAGUE	123
	STOCKHOLM	141
	BERLIN	153
COME AND GO	TOKYO	171
	KYOTO	182
	DELHI	189
	AGRA	206
	CAIRO	210
	ISTANBUL	233
	MINNEAPOLIS	257
AKNOWLEDGMENTS		258

PREFACE

The English travel writer Peter Fleming poked fun at travel writers who do not explain why they travel. "Was it boredom, business, or a broken heart that drove them so far afield?" he wrote in *One's Company,* his book about going to China in the 1930s. "We have a right to know. But they seldom tell us. They may vouchsafe a few complacent references to what they call their Wanderlust. But chiefly they trade on an air of pre-destination; they are lordly, inscrutable, mysterious. Without so much as a Hey Presto! or a Houp La! they whisk us from their native land to their exotic destination...."

I spent much of 1995 traveling. It was wanderlust in part. Restlessness is not necessarily a bad thing. Bruce Chatwin thought to wander was a form of bliss. We have to "up sticks and vanish into the blue" every now and then "to rediscover our humanity." Philanthropy was another reason. I was lucky enough to receive a grant. I did not head off into the blue as Chatwin prescribed. I did not go to the jungle, the desert, or the bush. I went to cities, Buenos Aires, Berlin, Delhi, Cairo, among others.

The kindness of friends, colleagues, and people at American embassies and consulates afforded many introductions. As an artist, I met many people in the arts. I also met teachers, business people, lawyers, journalists, cooks, shopkeepers. These strangers invited me into their homes, led me around their cities. My encounters with them fill much of this book.

In each city, I felt a deep-seated almost mystical desire to explore the center, the old square where the city grew up, to get to what Paul Rambali called "the nostalgic heart." Maybe it had something to do with being a restless American living in a modern country in a modern city where there was no center. I felt the hearts of ancient cities held some secret, some truth.

Day and night, I walked. Down streets of gracious and not so gracious buildings, through neighborhoods of bustle and of quiet, beauty and blight, plenty and want, serenity and pain. Markets, churches, museums, theaters, parks, cafés, harbors, I went everywhere. I wrote, drew, took photographs. In a state of constant exhilaration, I lived and breathed urban life. I was homesick often but never sick.

Laptops, cell phones, and the Internet have become fixtures in much of the world, but in the early 1990s they were new and magical, and also unsettling. Almost no one used e-mail then. I was curious about how these new electronic wonders would affect city life. Was human exchange going to be forever altered? Would computer screen become town square?

This is a travel book, but it is also a meditation on the tension between home and world, past and present, bricks and bits. It also, much to my surprise, turned into something more personal than I had intended. My mother died while I was traveling and this naturally found its way, as did other aspects of my life, into these pages.

The city at its best brings us together, on common ground with common plight, to talk and work and laugh and feel good, or sad, about being alive. The city enables us, if we let it, to get through the hearts of others to the hearts of ourselves. Technology and terrorism have changed the way we live. If cities now are more vulnerable and more fragile, they are also more cherished and protected. They seem more bracing and more necessary than ever as young and old we discover and rediscover their pleasures.

Topiary, Berlin

Museum, Santiago

THE OTHER AMERICA

MINNEAPOLIS	Place	17
LIMA	Buenos Dias / Two Squares / The Hour of Love / Café Olé	18
CUZCO	Coca / The Sleep of the Dead / The Nostalgic Heart / A Square Like This / The Ideal Place	28
QUITO	Stranger / Always Spring / Anchor / Secret / Double Helix	37
SANTIAGO	Upside-Down Stars / A Southern Place / Lunch with Palolo / Houses / The Computer Is the Piazza / Wed the Crowd / Loreto and Silvio / Alone	48
BUENOS AIRES	Spanish Lesson / Café Tortoni / Guillermo and Teatro Colon / The City of Beautiful Airs / The Crazy Years / To Eat the World / Stereotype	64
RIO DE JANEIRO	River of January / Dreamers / Eye Candy / The Art of Drinking in Rio / Ipanema	79
SALVADOR	Pelourinho / At Dada's / Past and Present / The Fruits of Bahia / Gift / Someone Else	86

Garden Chairs, Winter

MINNEAPOLIS

PLACE

The snow crunches beneath my feet, the wind stings. The light of the full moon on the hard snow is cold and blue yet somehow comforting. A siren wails, the dog sniffs, searching for smells in the frozen earth. Despite the cold, I walk an extra couple of blocks. The white clapboards of my house also look blue in the moonlight, blue and fragile.

A phone call from my father. My mother is in the hospital. It's too late to call her. Wendy is asleep by the fire, book and cat on her lap, Sarah laughs on the phone upstairs. I don't know if I agree with Pascal's idea that man's unhappiness is caused by his inability to sit quietly in a room. Nor necessarily with Bruce Chatwin's theory that man was born to wander, that aborigines, nomadic tribes, and inveterate travelers, like Chatwin himself, had a leg up on the sedentary world, burdened by property, possessions, and the past. Chatwin was obsessed and he carried his ideas too far, but he was on to something.

In a few days I'll be on my way to Peru. I sometimes think I am happiest when I am on the move. The phone rings again. It is my son, David, reminding me to bring his passport. I may be restless, but I care very much about place, about roots. I care about this city where I have lived in the same house for twenty years, where my children were born and raised, where my wife and friends and work are. I think the need for place, for history, for civilization is as powerful as the urge to flee them. I want to stay as much as I want to get away.

LIMA

BUENOS DIAS

When the plane leaps into the air, something in me leaps, some extra rush of excitement, trepidation, adrenaline. This is the first of a three-part solo journey around the world. Below, the Mississippi, half-frozen, winds through the flat snow-covered fields of Middle America. The other America lies far to the south. The unknown America. It's summer there. If this is the voyage of my dreams, why do I feel anxiety more than elation? Why do I think suddenly this is folly not adventure?

Sunlight filters through the arched roof of the terminal at O'Hare. It's a warm February day. CNN barks at the defenseless traveler. "News for people on the go." David, smiling broadly, arrives as planned from Maine. He will spend a week with me before I set out alone.

We arrive in Lima at dawn, cotton-mouthed, blinded by the sun on the tarmac. A rickety taxi takes us to our hotel in Miraflores. We cross the Rimac (the river whose Indian name the Spaniards mistook for Limac, which became Lima), pass through poor, raunchy neighborhoods that smell of exhaust and garbage. The taxi driver makes small talk in English. It's hot. A smiling, uniformed receptionist named Douchka hands me the key, a plastic card, to a clean, air-conditioned room with a view of a parking lot.

In a park, a man wearing a straw hat pulls puppets across a tiny stage while his leashed monkeys collect coins from children. People sit in the sun next to the church. On an ivy-covered cliff, we stare out at the blue Pacific. Even it seems foreign. The sun, normally a stranger to Lima, shines brightly. People hike up from the beach. Mothers herd gamboling children. Brown-skinned, black-haired boys with surfboards cool off in fountains. Skinny, scratching dogs dodge the big bicycles and the small cars. Next to a club, a man and woman play tennis on a red court. Signs warn of cholera.

We pass three women sitting on a bench. They look like they are related: a middle-aged woman flanked by two daughters. The woman smiles and asks me how old David is. Two boys kicking a soccer ball and eating popsicles grin at us. "*Buenos dias,*" they yell out. "*Buenos dias.*"

I can't sleep. A strange bed, a strange city. I turn on the light, open my book, Calvino's *Invisible Cities*. Reading is the best antidote for insomnia. "Arriving at each new city, the traveler finds again a past of his that he did not know he had: the foreignness of what you no longer are or no longer possess lies in wait for you in foreign, unpossessed places."

Surfers, Miraflores

TWO SQUARES

Plaza de Armas is the square of Pizarro, the Spanish conqueror who founded the city. A young man and woman loll in the grass near one of the square's big fountains. Their children, a small girl dressed in a bubble gum pink dress and two older boys dressed in slacks and white shirts, play in the midday sun. It's Sunday. Families like this are clustered throughout the square.

On one side of the square is the government palace, on another the eighteenth-century cathedral recently painted colonial yellow. (The trend in South America is to make the colors of the old squares historically correct.) Inside the church are Pizarro's remains, but when David pushes at the door it doesn't open. The balcony of the archbishop's palace next door is grand and strange. It's made of dark ornately carved wood. Across from the church is the town hall.

A few minutes away is the huge Plaza San Martin, the square of the liberator. It is surrounded by long, formidable mud red colonial buildings. Around San Martin's statue in the scruffy dirt and grass indolent men talk, sleep, pass the time. There is something slightly menacing about the vast treeless plaza. We have lunch in the elegant Hotel Bolivar that overlooks the square. The waiter in coat and tie is formal and glum.

We stop at other colonial sites: the Torre Tagle Palace with its massive wooden balconies, the San Pedro Church, the San Francisco Church. In the latter, we find a lovely cloister swarming with scrawny cats, vaulted ceilings made of wood carved in geometric patterns, rooms of dark religious paintings, and a maze of dank, smelly catacombs lined with the skulls and bones of ancient dead. Outside the church a *campesino* boy and a blind man sell candy and soft drinks and photocopied "guides" to the church.

In Barranco, we walk under the *Puente de los Suspiros* (Bridge of Sighs) and down a cobblestone street into a romantic neighborhood of gardens and charming old buildings. It's full of people, many going to and from the beach. This is the barrio of artists and bars and balloon sellers. We walk along a dusty path through a park lined with hibiscus and large yellow irises. Families lounge in the grass on the square, lovers, ever present, nuzzle in the shade. Crowded buses roll by, young boys hanging out the door, yelling at waiting passengers.

Lima is an old-fashioned place, primitive and poor, tactile and sensual. There is the smell of things cooking on the street. It is hot and dusty and listless. Spry, black-haired children are everywhere. As are soldiers and police. The dignified colonial buildings speak of past power and wealth. The city is proud of its Spanish ties. The heart of Lima is like old tapestry, once beautiful, now faded, tattered. Reading about plundering conquistadors and the brutality of the colonial era takes some of the charm out of the old churches and mansions. The Spanish craved gold so much the Incas thought they ate it. On my map are the Avenue of the Conquistadors and the Avenue of the Liberator. If many cherish their colonial heritage, many still suffer from it.

We have drinks with Adrianne and Morgan, a young American couple, and then join two Peruvians, Martine and his girlfriend, Ligia, at a restaurant in Barranco. Adrianne and Morgan are working with Martine to help computerize the stock exchange. We eat fish beneath an arbor. The night is mild. Martine orders wine and in a gruff but friendly voice launches into a history of the modern presidency in Peru.

Fujimori, he says, is popular because he vanquished both Shining Path and inflation, for the time being at least. About the border dispute with Ecuador, which is dominating the news, he says, "They are the aggressor, but the international media says we are." There is no real solidarity with other South American countries just competition. "Chile is the strongest now."

I mention the writer Maria Vargas Llosa. "We are angry with Llosa for leaving Peru after he lost the election," Martine says. "Peruvians are very political. America is more stable so Americans are less political." We talk about the water shortage in Lima.

Square, Barranco

Lima

Adrianne says she got sick after eating ceviche in a fancy restaurant and had to be rushed to the hospital.

"Should we order another bottle of wine?" I ask.

"Tell me about your art, David," Martine says across the table. "I suppose you are one of those abstract artists. Have you ever tried to expose yourself in New York?"

THE HOUR OF LOVE

"Where is the *sala erotica*?" I ask.

We have just walked through the white-washed hacienda of Rafael Lorca Herrera, admiring his vast collection of Indian ceramics and jewelry. A tiny soulful-looking man leads us outside past masses of bougainvillea to a long narrow windowless room. Standing by the door, like host and hostess, is a small ceramic man with a tremendous erection and a small ceramic woman with a tremendous vagina. They set the tone, to put it mildly. The room is a graphic, if not clinical, portrayal of carnality in clay.

There are dozens of red-glazed couples coupling. This is the work of the Mochica, dating from the first centuries after Christ. There is nothing pornographic or prurient about the pieces. They show not pleasure so much as straightforward depiction of coitus. Many of them are engaged in anal sex. Historians think this may have been a form of birth control.

"I don't think you would find a museum like this in the U.S.," David says.

Traffic on the way to Miraflores is heavy. Dust lifts off the patchwork streets, most of which are under repair or in need of it. The taxi driver winds his way through the crowded streets, turning often trying to find a quicker route. "There are forty-three barrios in Lima," he says. The barrio of the wealthy, the barrio of the poor ("*ni dinero*"), the barrio of the embassies.

Street vendors are everywhere, *campesinos* who have fled the farms and mountains and villages for a better life and have turned Lima into a refugee camp, a third-world city of shantytowns and struggle. At stop lights, barefoot boys and women in felt bowler hats and wide skirts come to our window with things to sell: plastic hangers, rolls of toilet paper, copies of *Architectural Digest*.

"Miraflores is a nice barrio," the driver says as he pulls up in front of our hotel. With its parks and lively shops and its perch on a cliff above the ocean, Miraflores has a Mediterranean flavor. Mario Vargas Llosa wrote lovingly about growing up here in the forties: "The barrio in Miraflores was innocent: a parallel family, a mixed tribe where you learned to smoke, dance, play sports, and open your heart to girls. The concerns were not very elevated; they came down to enjoying yourself to the hilt every holiday and every summer. The great pleasures were surfing and playing soccer, dancing the mambo gracefully and switching couples after awhile."

In the Parc del Amor overlooking the ocean is an immense, klunky sculpture of two half-prone lovers. They look a little like Picasso's thick-limbed neoclassical figures. Around it are real lovers, black-haired girls and boys knotted on serpentine mosaic benches.

". . . flesh . . . at the hour of love must have the tender abundance that appears to be just about to overflow yet remains firm, supple, resilient as ripe fruit and freshly kneaded dough, that soft texture Italians call *morbidezza*, a word that sounds lustful even when applied to bread." Llosa again. This is from *In Praise of the Stepmother*. It always seem to be the hour of love in Lima.

Lovers, Parc del Amor

CAFE OLE

David and I walk through a long grove of ancient olive trees in the barrio of San Isidro. We pass a little theater in a park. Hummingbirds feed by a pond. There are ice cream vendors, children playing, and tangled couples amid the gnarled trees. We find a bench in the shade and read for awhile.

We have a long dinner outside at Café Olé. The restaurant is modern and chic, unlike anything we have seen in Lima. We hear American voices, people talking on cell phones. A man in a double-breasted mango suit chats with two women at the bar. We talk of Sarah, the almost empty nest, college life, politics, tennis, Lima, the crowd. I tell my old travel stories.

David brings tears to my eyes with his hilarious replay of my shock at the $100 phone call we just made to Wendy and Sarah. "Do you love your wife and daughter, Señor Coggins?" he says with a heavy Spanish accent, imitating the hotel clerk, to whom I complained.

"Yes, yes, of course, I love my wife and daughter," he says, imitating me.

"Then a hundred dollars is nothing. It is fortunate dogs cannot talk."

"Why is that?"

"It would have cost another fifty dollars. You do have a dog, Señor Coggins?"

We walk afterward in the olive grove. It's a warm night. The air is filled with the cooing of doves and lovers. And two gringos chuckling.

"It makes such a funny story," I say, "it's almost worth the price."

"A hundred dollars is nothing, Señor Coggins," David says. "To talk to your wife and daughter. All the way from Lima. What is the price of love, Señor Coggins?"

CUZCO

COCA

Paper cups of *maté de coca* and oxygen tanks greet us in the Cuzco airport. At 11,000 feet, Cuzco takes some getting used to. *Soroche*, altitude sickness, is a very real thing. The road into town is lined with cheerful yellow broom flower. The surrounding hills are green, the air fresh from an earlier rain. We drink *maté* in the hotel lobby, but it doesn't help much. We're short of breath and our heads are starting to hurt. David, feeling queasy, decides to lay low for awhile.

The Plaza de Armas was called the Weeping Square because Incas mourned their dead here. People and dogs crisscross the square in the rain. It has trees, fountains, benches, and is of a human scale. Flanked by stone churches and arcades full of *campesinos* in bright wool, the square draws you in. Results of recent elections are papered across the long wall of one arcade. People pause to study them and to talk.

The streets of heavy Inca stone and buildings with red-tiled roofs are set off nicely by the green hills. In a convent I am given an impromptu tour by two girls, who, trying out their English, describe the Inca women who lived here and worshipped the sun god.

I drink more *maté* at the hotel. I wonder if I shouldn't chew it as the *indigenas* do. Crack cocaine is made from leaves like the ones in the tea. The U.S. government wants South American countries to stop growing coca because crack is destroying so many lives in our inner cities. Coca is sacred to Andean Indians. They chew it every day and have for thousands of years. They consume it the way we consume coffee and tea. They chew it to fight off pain, sickness, and exhaustion. They put coca leaves in the coffins of their dead.

Church, Plaza de Armas

Cuzco

THE SLEEP OF THE DEAD

The setting of Machu Picchu is almost more spellbinding than the place itself. The ruins sit on a mountain plateau ringed by steep dusty green peaks bathed in clouds. The peaks rise up from Machu Picchu (*Quechua* for old peak) across gorges, one of which the Urubamba courses swiftly through. We can see the river far below. Just to the north is Huayna Picchu, or young peak, a "great dark cone," as Peter Matthiessen calls it, which "stands guard over the roofless city, where grasses blow and brilliant flowers bloom in the dead houses."

Drifting clouds add to the mystical atmosphere as does the green and the dampness. Everything is softened, muted, dreamy. Except, of course, for the ruins themselves, the heavy gray geometric stones which were used to make the maze of terraces, temples, and rooms. No one has figured out how the stones were transported (the Incas did not have draft animals or the wheel), how they were made so smooth, and how, most mysterious and marvelous of all, the Incas managed to get them to fit so neatly and elegantly together. Machu Picchu is eloquent in its silence.

We may not be sure of the technology, but we know a tremendous amount of manpower was needed to haul the thousand-pound stones. Pablo Neruda, in his famous epic poem, sympathizes with those who built Machu Picchu. Was it built, he asks, "on a groundwork of rags?" He honors the sweat and toil of the anonymous laborers: "I come to speak for your dead mouths."

I tell David how the American Hiram Bingham was led to these ruins hidden in jungle by a *campesino* in the early twentieth century. Theories vary, but one holds that Machu Picchu was built in the fifteenth century and abandoned in the sixteenth and until Bingham was unknown to the world at large. The Spanish never found it. Though extensive farming was done at Machu Picchu (indeed some say its main function was to provide coca for the upper crust of Cuzco), most experts think it was

mainly used for religious ceremony. Standing near the Temple of the Sun, listening to the eerie sound of the *quena*, gazing at llamas feeding and clouds swirling around, I am overwhelmed by the spiritual power of the place.

Back in Cuzco, David and I have dinner on the mezzanine of a restaurant facing Plaza de Armas. We eat meat grilled on a small tin of coals set on our table. There is a political rally in the square. A band plays while a small group of people parade around holding placards. In our room, we open the door to the courtyard and fall asleep to the sound of a fountain. I don't know about my son, but I sleep the sleep of the dead.

Pisac Market

THE NOSTALGIC HEART

The Pisac market is earthy and vibrant. *Campesino* women in thick skirts and sweaters squat on the cobblestoned square. All around are blankets and sheets of plastic piled with fruits and vegetables, baskets and sacks, stout as the women themselves, filled with earth's bounty. Cherries, bananas, onions, avocados, cheese, corn, lettuces, carrots, yucca, chilies. You want to stick your hands into the sacks and scoop up the olives or nuts or beans like water. Potatoes are everywhere.

The women have a dignity about them despite the long girlish braids hanging from their jaunty straw hats. One woman's black braids are tied together at the bottom and form a giant oval on her back. Their broad faces, the color of leather, are weathered and scarred, their teeth are long and stained, their eyes wise and sad. They laugh and talk quietly among themselves. The young ones nurse their babies.

Isaias, our guide, buys a couple of ears of *choclo.* They have big white kernels and are boiled in the husk in a big vat. "I love eating it in the market," he says. We walk through the covered stalls near a big pisonay tree. We look at woven blankets. "The old ones are *más finitas,*" Isaias says. "More fine." We bargain with one vendor who shows us prices on a calcuator. Most of the vendors are women. The men drink *chicha* in doorways and around tables on the perimeter of the plaza.

On the way back, Isaias stops the van on a hillside. We look down at Cuzco sitting in the valley. Gray clouds roll over the green and red mountains. In the center of town is the glowing green plaza, the nostalgic heart, around which the red-tiled buildings and narrow streets of stone come to rest. "My favorite view," Isaias says. "But the city has grown so much. I remember when the airport used to be next to the Cusquena brewery. The Incas built Cuzco in the shape of a puma. It doesn't look like a puma now."

A SQUARE LIKE THIS

On Cuzco's main square soldiers lower the red and white Peruvian flag in front of the cathedral. There is much pomp and trumpet blowing, completely undermined by the utter lack of seriousness on the part of the ragtag soldiers. A young boy falls into their ranks and goosesteps along with them as they march off down the street. The cathedral is closed so we hike up to the bohemian quarter of San Blas. We see along the way the famous twelve-angled Inca stone in the wall of a former palace.

On the charming if austere *plazoleta* of San Blas is a small museum of religious art and a simple church with an elaborate wooden pulpit, carved, legend has it, by a man after he was cured of leprosy. I climb some steps and look down on the small square. Children ride bicycles around the fountain, a few people sit on benches, reading the paper or dozing. A dog follows a man in a suit. Two women talk in a doorway. There are few cars. It's a quiet place, removed from the center of town, but it's a magnet for the people in the neighborhood, a place for them to talk, to sit, to play, to be a part of the world. Every neighborhood should have a square like this.

This is the kind of square that Christopher Alexander would approve of. Alexander and his colleagues at the Center for Environmental Structure in Berkeley wrote a series of books promoting a new kind of architecture that enables people to design their own houses and towns. In *A Pattern Language*, they write: "A town needs public squares; they are the largest, most public rooms, that the town has. But when they are too large, they look and feel deserted." They even go so far as to say that the diameter of the perfect square should be about sixty feet. "At this diameter, people often go to them, they become favorite places, and people feel comfortable there."

Plazoleta, San Blas

THE IDEAL PLACE

I love big cities, but I wonder if maybe a smaller city, one with the beauty of Cuzco, isn't the ideal place. I remember J.B. Priestley's description of his "secret dream" in Paul Fussell's *Abroad*:

> . . . a place with the dignity and style of a city, but reasonably small and clean, with genuine country only half an hour's walk from its center, its single but superb theater, its opera house, its symphony orchestra, its good restaurant always filled with friends. One little civilized place full of persons, with no nameless mob, no huge machinery of publicity, no glaring metropolis. . . . Everything small but of fine quality, cozily within reach, and means and ends in sight of each other. . . .

Sounds a little like Minneapolis.

Evelyn Waugh's vision of urban perfection is also quoted in Fussell's book. Among other things, it includes "shady boulevards; kiosks for flowers and cigars and illustrated papers; the hotel terrace and the cafes; the baroque church built by seventeenth-century missionaries; the bastions of the old fort; the bandstand in the square, standing amidst fountains and flowering shrubs...."

I could live in either Priestley's or Waugh's imaginary town. I wonder if I could live in a village far removed from everything. If it had the age, setting, and beauty of Machu Picchu, perhaps I could. If it had a good wine store and a good bookstore. And a nice square.

STRANGER

The tiny bar is full of photos of old Hollywood stars. A sign on the wall says in English: "The same procedure as last year." American rock and roll is on the radio. I order a bottle of Ecuadorian beer and smoke my first cigarette in a week. My eye lights on a picture of Clark Gable.

"What am I doing here?" The traveler's age-old question. David has flown back to the U.S. The woman who was supposed to meet me at the airport didn't show. I am sitting in a hotel in Quito on a gray February afternoon toward the end of the twentieth century. I do not know a single person on this entire continent. The weeks before my trip were a flurry of letters, faxes, and phone calls. I left with a long list of people (artists, teachers, lawyers, journalists, businessmen) I hoped would give me a real sense of what life is like in Quito, Buenos Aires, Rio de Janeiro, and the other cities I'm visiting.

Until I got here I didn't know how much time these people would spend with me or how they would take to a gringo stranger who doesn't speak Spanish. I finish the beer and go back to my room. Moments later, the phone rings. "Mr. Coggins, someone in the lobby for you."

Downstairs, I meet Patricia von Buchwald, her husband, Javier, and their young son. "I'm so glad you are here," Patricia says. "I'm sorry we could not meet you at the airport. Would you like to come with us now to see the old city?"

Patricia talks excitedly, mostly in Spanish. Javier translates for her. We drive through narrow streets in the rain. Patricia is a curator of education and culture for the city. "I lived for seven years as a child in the United States," she says. "But my English is not good anymore." She is a vibrant, charismatic woman.

Her husband is handsome and, like his wife, eager to show me Quito. The old town is a forest of whitewashed buildings. The streets are crowded. We find a place to park

The Old City

and walk in the rain across the main square, Plaza Independencia. We poke our heads into the cathedral where a wedding is taking place. Quito's colonial center has been designated a world historic site by UNESCO, Patricia tells me. "Slowly we are getting the money to fix up the old center. It was in bad shape. We have done churches and government buildings and the square itself."

"They look beautiful."

"People live again in the old center," Javier says. "The new mayor just moved here." The rain drives us back to the car.

I ask if there are things for people to do.

"More and more," Javier says.

It's Saturday night. I wipe the fog from the window and look out. Despite the rain, Quito has the bustling, electric feel of a Saturday night. Sitting in the warmth of the car with this family I've just met, I feel oddly, in some small way, a part of the city.

ALWAYS SPRING

Sunday morning. My room is filled with the sound of roosters and buses. Miroslav Kubes arrives in his jeep. We are going up in the hills above the city. Trained as an architect, Miroslav spent three years at the Virginia Polytechnic Institute on a Fulbright scholarship. He works for an American oil company. We drive through the San Marcos barrio, looking at old buildings, many of them being restored. Freshly painted in bold colors (the colors of the sun, of South America), the houses and shops beam with charm and cheer.

On the way up the mountain, we pass Cimo de la Libertad, an ugly concrete structure commemorating a battle between Spain and Ecuador. We also pass an immense sculpture of the Virgin. It sits on *El Panecillo* (The Little Bun) and is visible throughout the city. In one small square a man is roasting a pig. "*Asado*," Miroslav says. "People in the neighborhood come and buy pieces of pork from him."

After driving up a dirt road, we stop and get out. "I love this view," Miroslav says. "On one side is city, on the other country." Quito sits in a valley surrounded by mountains. To the west is the volcano Pichincha (though silent now, it has destroyed the city more than once). In the distance barely visible is the snowy cone of Cotopaxi. A handful of clouds dot the pristine sky. The air is sweet and mild. "Quito has the best weather in the world," Miroslav says. "It's always spring. We are only miles from the equator, but we are at 3,000 meters so it never gets really hot or really cold."

It is easy to see where old Quito ends and modern Quito begins. Miroslav points out Parque El Ejido, Avenida Amazonas, *El Panecillo*, the wealthy neighborhoods. The country view, a broad valley of farms and mountains beyond, stretches as far as the eye can see. Miroslav picks some of the pretty flowers that grace the hillside. "This is a kind of passion flower called *taxo*," he says. "This is *guanto*. It's a trumpet flower."

"You are a naturalist as well as an architect."

We wind our way back through quaint neighborhoods of narrow streets, old men, take-out windows, and dogs. We stop at the seventeenth-century Guapulo Church perched poetically on the banks of the Machangara River. "Are you hungry?" Miroslav asks. "I know a good place for Sunday lunch." Within minutes we are sitting in a restaurant filled with light and pretty families in nice clothes.

"I'm afraid to eat ceviche," I confess.

"Nonsense," Miroslav says and orders a ceviche of shrimp.

We talk about the border dispute with Peru. Miroslav refers to it as "the war." Ecuador is angry at Peru because Peru has seized much of its country over the years, including Ecuador's access to the Amazon. "Peru has a warlike mentality. Ecuador is peace-loving. Carnival has been canceled. Everyone must give up at least two days pay. There is an additional two percent tax if you buy a new car. All proceeds go to financing the war. We are very patriotic."

He tells me about his family. His mother and father, originally from Czechoslovakia, met in Ecuador and when he was a young boy they lived on a farm in the jungle. "Quito is beautiful, but the next time you come you must go to the jungle."

ANCHOR

Another tour of colonial Quito, this time with Victoria Carrasco and her brother Santiago. Quitenos are proud of the old center, the historic heart of their city. Quitenos have a strong sense of place. When people visit me in Minneapolis, I always want to take them to the center of the city, but it doesn't exist. We go to the business district or to the warehouse district and maybe to an old mill on the banks of the Mississippi, but there is no one place that is the anchor, that gives you a sense of really being in the city or of the city's past.

Witold Rybczynski says in his book *City Life* that most cities have hallmark places that clearly identify them, that are their symbolic centers. Sometimes they are monuments like the Eiffel Tower or buildings like Buckingham Palace, but usually they are large public spaces like Piazza San Marco in Venice or Red Square in Moscow.

In America, Rybczynski writes, the center of the city is likely to be a street corner, like Hollywood and Vine in Los Angeles or Times Square in New York, which is really an intersection not a square. He thinks it has something to do with our constant mobility and our dependence on cars. It could also be because our cities, unlike cities in Europe, are always changing. If buildings are continually getting torn down or turned into something else, at least the streets remain the same. Still can anyone get excited thinking Nicollet and Seventh is the heart of Minneapolis?

Rybczynski, along with the late landscape historian J. B. Jackson, whom he cites in his book, think the notion of a city having a center and well-defined physical places has been "replaced by something else—something diffuse, amorphous, and held together by a system of roads and highways...and telephone wires, television cables, and computer links." In *A Sense of Place, A Sense of Time,* Jackson writes that with a few exceptions, North American cities "not only are lacking in architectural variety, they are lacking in landmarks and in unique neighborhoods." Foreign visitors often wonder "how we who live in the midst of such monotony can have any sense of place."

Victoria and I have a drink in her apartment while waiting for her brother. Victoria is a weaver, a tall, quiet woman in her forties who lives alone. She shows me some of her weavings and the big loom in the room where she works. We talk for awhile in her living room with its wonderful view of the city. She tells me she has spent the day hiking in the mountains.

Her brother arrives and we take his car. Santiago is a solid man, quite a bit older than Victoria, and has the confident air of a man of accomplishment. Victoria tells me that her brother is the secretary of science and technology for the government. "Sort of like being the head of the NSF in your country," Santiago tells me. "As a matter of fact, I just came back from Washington."

"Were you there on business?"

"I was asking for money," he says and laughs.

SECRET

The streets of old Quito are so crowded they are almost impassable. Beneath the soft blue morning sky, office workers, old women, soldiers, policemen, children with backpacks flood the narrow *calles*. Taxis and buses spew exhaust, shopkeepers unlock doors. "Life in the city is real," Patricia says over her shoulder. "It keeps the old town from becoming a museum."

We weave in and out, sometimes on the sidewalk, sometimes on the street. *Campesino* vendors have carts on every corner and every plaza. Dozens of shoeshine boys prowl the cobblestones. Quito, like Lima, suffers from an invasion of the rural poor. "We don't know what to do with all these people. There is no work, no place for them to live."

Patricia takes me to La Campania de Jesus. "This is the most beautiful church in South America. One and a half tons of gold were used here," Patricia says as we stand before ravishing baroque woodwork. Paintings cover the vaulted ceiling, murals by School of Quito painters adorn the walls. Quito is rich in churches. There are almost ninety of them. And the churches in Quito are rich, at least the colonial ones. Their splendor throws the hand-to-mouth existence of the people on the street into greater relief. It's hard to refuse the beggar at the door after seeing a church's lavish interior.

We stop at the *sala capitular* in La Iglesia San Agustin where the declaration of independence from Spain was signed in 1809 and at the courtyard of the presidential palace to see the mural painted by Guayasamin, Ecuador's most renowned painter. "Closed," a young soldier tells us. "Because of the war."

"Come, I want to show you something special," Patricia says. We enter a building under restoration. "This was Quito's first hospital. We are making it into our new offices." We pass through courtyards in disarray. Indians have squatted in one. Clothes hang on the railing of a balcony drying in the sun. Kids play near stalks of corn growing by a fountain. I follow Patricia into a chapel where a man is applying gold leaf to an angel's wing. The angel is part of a large carving of religious figures. There are ladders and buckets and tools lying around. I want to say something about the squatting Indians, maybe even something about the plight of the poor, but instead I say how beautiful the carving is.

Without a word Patricia ushers me into a stairway. She climbs some stairs. "Follow me." It's pitch black and the stairs are winding and narrow. She opens a door and we come out on the roof into glaring sunlight. "This is my secret place," she says, spreading her arms as if to embrace the city below. I look out over the red-tiled roofs, church towers, and busy streets.

"It's wonderful," I say, a little breathless.

"I love it up here," she says, walking over to the edge.

I'm a little stunned and flattered, too, I think. "It's nice of you to bring me here."

Patricia's dark eyes hold mine for a second. "My secret," she says and smiles.

I don't know what to say.

Back on solid ground, we part company. I think about Patricia in the taxi on the way back to the hotel. The driver speaks then makes a face when I tell him I don't understand. He pulls over and buys two small Ecuadorian flags from a man on the sidewalk. He speaks to me again, waving one of the flags. I glance at his face in the rear view mirror. He is looking at me, first sternly, then quizzically. Is he telling me something or asking?

Church Crucifix

DOUBLE HELIX

Battered candy-colored buses circle big El Ejido park in modern Quito. In the shabby park, kids play soccer, women sell grilled corn. Some boys toss carnival water balloons at a group of girls in blazers and skirts walking home from school. Signs on the corners of Avenida Rio Amazonas say "Don't take drugs" and "Protect against AIDS (SIDA)." A big cardboard box full of letters is strapped on the back wheel of a mailman's bicycle; from the center bar hangs a sign that says *Correos Del Ecuador*. An old *campesino* lady goes from street to street trying to sell the two or three orchids she clutches in her hand. To the west, green, serene Pichincha stands out against an ethereal blue sky.

In front of a clothing store on the fashionable Calle Juan Leon Mera, a woman in a dress stands guard with a rifle slung over her shoulder. Armed guards are in front of most of the stores. The shady street is full of galleries, *artesanís* stores, and antique shops. The Libri Mundi Bookstore has the charm and eccentricity of a true bookstore, including a bearded man who knows where everything is.

I have lunch in a café with blond tables and big umbrellas set in a garden. Sitting across from me are two well-groomed young Ecuadoran men looking at a fat art book they bought at the bookstore. Rowdy students at one table talk about going down the Amazon in a mix of languages — German, American, Spanish. A young woman sits by herself, nursing a cup of coffee and reading a paperback with the cover torn off. She has long fingernails and smokes self-consciously. She seems unmistakably American.

The label on the bottle of my cerveza reads "*Bebida de moderacion.*" It would be nice to be having a beer with my son. I too am unmistakably American, I suppose. I have the American double helix of wanderlust and homesickness.

It's midnight. Streets in the working-class neighborhood around my hotel are quiet and smell of garbage and wood smoke. I hear soft salsa music. In front of one dark house, some people are having a party. A fire burns behind a falling down fence. A

Under the Hood, Parc El Ejido

skinny boy with a bottle in his hand sways with a girl wearing a wide-brimmed hat. At least someone is celebrating carnival.

    I cross the street. Three skinny dogs pass by sniffing one another. One stops to sniff my leg. "What do I smell like?" I say out loud. "Do I have a strange smell?" The dog looks at me, cocks its head then moves on with a funny crooked gait.

    Back in my hotel roon, I turn on the television for a moment. On one channel is a movie. The reception is not good and the voices are in Spanish, but there is no mistaking the faces of Goldie Hawn and Warren Beatty. The smell of rain drifts through the window. I hear the rustling of palm trees and, in the distance, the howling of a dog.

S A N T I A G O

UPSIDE-DOWN STARS

As the plane leaves Quito, the Andes are staggeringly beautiful. Sloping farm fields of soothing green give way to forest, which gives way to the long spine of red brown mountains. We fly over volcanoes. Every now and then a snow-capped peak punctures a cloud. Soon we are above the ocean. It is five hours to Santiago.

Es un dia hermoso. It is a lovely day. The Pacific is a brilliant cobalt blue below my window. To the east, the mountains are endless, imperious, but as the planes flies farther off coast, the blue edge of the sky and the blue edge of the sea melt into one. The horizon and the mountains disappear, leaving only a shimmering veil of blue. The mind shifts from reality to dream, helped along perhaps by the pleasant meal and genteel service on board: a table cloth, a fresh flower, wine poured from a bottle, a tray of *empanadas*, perhaps even by the cover of the menu showing a melancholy leopard languishing by a jungle river.

I am brought back to reality by the hefty woman sitting next to me. Gleaming with jewels, bright makeup, and painted nails, she guzzles food, wine, and Coke, gets up repeatedly, and sits with the force of a small bomb. She presses her large features against a tiny mirror and sighs. She smiles at me.

Santiago is greener, newer, and more familiar than I expected. My hotel in the center of town has a view of the Santa Lucia Hill. French windows open on to a busy street bordered by palm trees. The view of the park from the rooftop restaurant, where I have dinner, is even better. I eat *pastel de choclo*, the Chilean national dish. It's a kind of shepherd's pie of meat and corn. I drink Chilean wine. I eat alone, which heightens the feeling of being in a foreign place.

For dessert I have a peach. Eating a peach for me is like climbing into a time machine. I am cast back to South Carolina, to the baskets piled high with peaches at the orchard where my uncle worked, to my grandmother's hand-churned silky peach

Post Office, Plaza de Armas

ice cream that I ate with my brothers and cousins on my grandfather's farm during summers in the fifties. I don't know which is more real: the sweet, voluptuous peach of my past or the small, hard peach I am served for dessert.

The Parque Forestal parallels the Mapocho River. It's a balmy night. The piecrust mansion in the park used to be the American Embassy before it was transplanted to a modern windowless fortress in the suburbs. I look up in the Chilean sky. I am a long way from home and the stars are upside-down.

A SOUTHERN PLACE

The Andes are the color of terracotta, of chili powder, of sunburn. The view of the mountains from the top of Santa Lucia hill is worth the long climb. The hill is in a park full of leafy paths and lovely fountains and squares. It was here that the Spanish conquistador Pedro de Valdivia founded the city in the sixteenth century. He came, I read in a guidebook, with "a motley assortment of adventurers and a sole woman, his lover, Ines de Suarez." Now, I think, *santiaguinos* follow in the conquistador's path as lovers more than as adventurers. Couples embrace on benches in the park. At the foot of the hill people dip their hands and faces in the big baroque fountain on the Terraza Neptuno before returning to the hot city streets.

Santiago is an earthy place, a southern place. It is a saw stuck in an orange squash, lovers entwined in grass steps away from clanging traffic, white ice cream melting on a child's brown hand, the smoke of a bus blackening a crossroads, the smell of fresh fish on ice. It is the Mapocho River, in winter a brown gruel flowing swiftly in a shallow canal. It is a gardener's sweat-stained khakis, the blue and pink post office.

Santiago is the Mercado Central. I walk through the market on this hot Saturday afternoon, starting in the main hall, a nineteenth-century, English-made wrought iron building. Then by the stalls that sprawl across a bridge on the Mapocho and into another big hall. There are stands of watermelons, buckets of bullfrogs, hanging pigs' heads, fish galore.

People come not only to shop but to eat. They sit shoulder to shoulder at counters hunched over plates singing with food. At the Pergola de las Flores, men make huge wreaths of roses and white carnations for gravesites. It smells of the greenhouse. Beyond the market next to the river stands the handsome turn-of-the-century Estacion Mapocho, no longer a place for trains but for culture. Inside the walls of lacy ironwork a tent has been pitched as a temporary theater.

I have dinner with Josefina Guillesanti and José Mingo. We eat in the kitchen of their big modern apartment. Josefina is an artist; she is pretty and quiet. José works for Concho y Toro, the famous Chilean winery; he has a beard, is small and talkative. They lived in Milan for a while and have traveled extensively in Asia. Josefina shows me her paintings. José talks about marketing wine. We talk about life in our respective cities.

"I was in Minneapolis once," José says.

"Did you like it?"

"It was cold."

"When were you there?"

"July."

Terraza Neptuno

LUNCH WITH PALOLO

Martine is naked except for white jelly sandals. He splashes in the kiddie pool and chases Flora around the garden and the bright plastic toys on the patio. The children laugh and yelp. The little boy stops suddenly and begins to pee. "Martine!" Palolo yells and cups his hand beneath his son's tiny penis. I look at Ignacia. She laughs and puffs on her cigarette.

We sit down to lunch. "Have you had *pastel de choclo*?" he asks. "You must know our wines. They are very good, don't you think?" Pablo "Palolo" Valdez is an artist. Slight with short gray-flecked hair and a twinkle in his eye, he lived for awhile in New York. "I am planning a trip to Germany and to the Venice Biennale. It is very hard to sell paintings in Santiago." He has a playful, devil-may-care attitude. He has invited his friend Ignacia and her daughter Flora to join us.

He shows me a catalog of his work and an article in a glossy magazine with photos of his home and studio enclosed behind walls in an old neighborhood not far from downtown Santiago. When I arrived, a uniformed maid escorted me through the garden and into a high-ceilinged room and gave me a fruit drink. Half an hour later, Palolo appeared and introduced himself.

After the long lunch, Palolo lights a joint and invites us into his studio. "My neighbors are finally getting used to me," he says with a grin. The bull is his motif. Sculptures of bulls in metal and stone lurk in the garden. In the spacious studio are several works in progress. Styrofoam molds of bulls' heads lie on tables.

We have coffee in the garden where bougainvillea spills over the pergola like a waterfall. "I just came back from a kayaking trip in the south of Chile," Palolo says. "It is full of lakes and forests. Very beautiful. There is ice in the ocean. My kayak overturned and I almost died. I had to be rescued at sea." He teases Flora, flirts with Ignacia. I like his light-heartedness (he is more satyr than bull) and admire the way he has created a private world of work and pleasure, his studio a lush garden away from his house.

HOUSES

La Chascona is the name of the house Pablo Neruda designed and named after Matilde Urrutia, the woman he lived with in his last years. La Chascona means "woman with tousled hair." Ignacia, Flora, and I arrive at the steps of the poet's blue house in Bellavista just before it closes. Built on three levels (with three bars) in the side of a hill, it is a disjointed assemblage of terraces, gardens, and small uninspiring rooms. If the architecture disappoints, the furnishings — Neruda was an inveterate collector — do not. His touch is everywhere. Paintings by friends, Mexican dishes, shells, the first edition of Diderot's Encyclopedia, the framed Nobel Prize. There is a secret passageway and in the driveway, a Citroën, his last car.

"It's not bad," Ignacia says as we leave, "but you should see his house in Isla Negra. By the sea. Much more interesting." We stop for coffee. The Bellavista barrio with its streets of acacias and one-story pastel houses is inviting. "It used to be very nice," Ignacia says. "Very bohemian with cafés and theaters and galleries. Now it's too popular, too touristy. Too many drinkers."

"English is not in my head in summer," Flora says to me from the back seat of the car as her mother weaves through rush hour traffic toward her parents' home. Until now, Flora has spoken only Spanish.

"She goes to an English language school," Ignacia says.

I tell Flora she speaks English well. She is a tall, skinny, hyperactive eleven-year old. "You are very pretty and you like to talk."

"I talk in English now." And she does the rest of the way.

The Herrera house is in a prosperous suburb north of the city. With its heavy security, thick garden, pool, and view of sun setting over mountains, it could be in southern California. Except that the view also includes in the middle distance the house of Augusto Pinochet. After drinks with Raimundo Herrera, Ignacia's father (a cerebral man who tells me there are 500,000 English and 250,000 Spanish words), Ignacia and I drive back into the city through pleasant if unremarkable neighborhoods. We stop for gas. "We could be in the U.S.," I say, as we pull into a big, well-lit station.

"We are becoming so Americanized," Ignacia says. "Suburbs, fast food, baseball caps worn backward." We land in a dark, loud café for dinner. Ignacia works freelance in movie production. "I just worked on Kevin Costner's new movie," she says. "*Waterworld*. It was filmed on Easter Island. They spent 70 million dollars. Making it was a fiasco."

Ignacia has black hair and a husky voice. She is wearing leather pants and smokes hungrily. She just moved back to Santiago after living in Barcelona for ten years. She was married to a Spaniard and has been arguing with him over alimony and child support. "It's difficult for me right now. I want to move out of my parents' house. I'm sharing a room with Flora. Santiago is not a good place for a single woman. There are seven women to every man. And the government is bad. They don't do anything to help the poor. Nothing. Nada."

THE COMPUTER IS THE PIAZZA

"The city is a thing of the past," says Edmundo Fuenzalida. "What we have now is megapolis. Conurbanization." Edmundo is a professor of social sciences at Catholic University in Santiago. He lived and taught in Europe and the U.S. for many years. He has gray hair and an open face and is wearing a sport coat. We are sitting in a restaurant eating fish.

"In Renaissance Florence," Edmundo says, "the piazza fulfilled the need for people to come together, to shop, to eat, to do business. The technology was the architecture, the buildings forming the square. Today people use new technology, the computer, to interact. The computer is the piazza."

"Scary thought. Do you like Santiago?"

"I don't know Santiago anymore. I was away for twenty years and didn't recognize it when I came back."

"Do you want to stay in the city?"

"I am building a home in the country. What do you hope to find in old cities?"

"Life in older cities, older cultures seems more satisfying to me."

"I don't think you will find what you are looking for in the past."

"Will I find it in the future?"

"*Navigáre necésse est, vívere non est necésse.*"

WED THE CROWD

The sky is blue, the sun is hot. I merge with the throngs on Alameda Bernardo O'Higgins. Like Baudelaire's *flâneur*, I "wed the crowd." I am "the amateur of life who enters into the crowd as into an immense reservoir of electricity." I head for Plaza de Armas, Santiago's central square, which to my delight is alive and well. It has fountains, trees, pigeons, cafés, and lots of people.

I stroll among the shoeshine men, chess players, portrait sketchers, evangelists, balloon sellers, news vendors. I join people on a bench eating ice cream in the sun, listening to musicians in a bandstand. I establish my "house in the heart of the multitude, amid the ebb and flow of movement.... I am at the center of the world yet remain hidden from the world." I watch the parade of children and mothers who have bought school supplies at the stationery shops nearby. It's the end of February. Summer is coming to an end in Santiago. The crowd is strange and foreign yet I feel at home because these people feel at home.

I go into the big baroque church, then across the street into the blue post office. Inside the walls are pink. Light floods in through a skylight. Who would expect a post office to be so cheering? Down the street in the Museo Chileno de Arte PreColombino I wander through an exhibit of ancient ceramics made by the Indians of northern Chile. These people were rooted. The bowls they ate out of were made from the earth beneath their feet.

Edmundo's comments remind me of William Mitchell's book *City of Bits*. Mitchell, dean of the school of architecture at M.I.T., thinks that the Internet will create a whole new way of living. He says the same thing Edmundo says: the keyboard is his café. Mitchell says the Internet is antispacial. It has nothing to do with Piazza Navona or Copley Plaza. The city of the future, he writes, "will be unrooted to any definite spot on the surface of the earth. Its places will be constructed virtually by software instead of physically from stones and timbers, and they will be connected by logical linkages rather than by doors, passageways, and streets."

Kiosk, Plaza de Armas

If the Internet is antispacial, isn't it also ultimately antisocial? Doesn't it negate or greatly diminish the opportunity for human contact, the real not the virtual kind?

Unlike Plaza de Armas, Plaza de la Constitucion has little character. The immense presidential palace sits like a prison on one side of the square, banks and offices on the others. There are a few people on the square, sunning and reading, but the place is charmless, even bleak. I would much rather read the paper in the lively, colorful Plaza de Armas.

Proust says custom makes a room, or a place, inhabitable. J.B. Jackson believes "ritual repetition" gives a place meaning, doing something pleasant or memorable on a regular basis in a familiar spot with people you know, like going to a football game or a country fair or celebrating Thanksgiving. Sharing a sense of time connects us to a place and to each other.

I agree. But what might be called the "presence" of place — how it looks and feels — also connects us to it. Beauty is important but not mandatory. A place with presence has energy, surprise, elegance, tackiness, something that enlivens us, that makes us want to come back. It can be ancient or modern, though presence develops in places more often over time. Getting up from a bench, I walk quickly across Plaza de la Constitucion and back into the crowded streets.

Chess Players, Plaza de Armas

LORETO AND SILVIO

Loreto Zuniga is a striking woman with perfect white teeth who paints angry anti-Catholic paintings. She lives with Silvio Paredes, a musician, in a little house in Vitacura, a Santiago suburb. Most of her paintings are large and dominated by large black and white crosses and skeletal figures with tortured faces. The subject of her latest work is women. Crosses are juxtaposed with images and text from popular magazines. One has a woman with a facelift, another a Barbie doll.

"I work on social themes," she says. "Other women's work is soft. I don't do butterflies." I am struck by the contrast between Loreto's quiet demeanor and the intense rage in her work.

"Most art is commercial," Silvio says. He is a small, engaging man in his early thirties. "It goes with the sofa, looks good in fancy magazines." He studied engraving at art school. "Everything is an etching. Digging a grave. A hit on the arm leaves a bruise. All kinds of actions leave a mark." We drink beer as he prepares lunch. He walks twice to the corner store to buy more beer. I can't get over what an odd couple they are, odd but appealing. Loreto is tall, elegant, Silvio is short, boyish, quick to laugh.

From etching Silvio moved to music. "Sound on the ear is a kind of etching," he says. He is interested in ambient music, the sounds of everyday life, from the kitchen, for example, which he incorporates into his band's music. I tell him my ideas about the square. "The radio is a square," he says. "There is a square in every home. People sitting around listening to the radio as they would sit around a square. Everybody is listening to the same thing." Silvio used to record things from the radio to use in his music, but says his music is more high-tech now.

"It's transmusic," he says, becoming animated again. "We use the electronic synthesizer. We use pure sound or abstract sound to produce an emotion, to transform the listener, to open the listener up. It's a new way of listening. It works like a drug only it's healthy. The square now is when people come together for a performance and interact with the music."

ALONE

I buy a sandwich at the corner store and eat in my room. I phone home. Wendy and Sarah are tired of winter. "How is it down there?" they ask. I have coffee in a nearby café, then go for a walk in the pleasant Santiago night. The streets are quiet. *Four Weddings and a Funeral* is playing at the neighborhood movie house. I pass antique stores, used bookstores, cafés. I come upon the small church I passed on an earlier walk. The doors are closed now, but then they were open to the street. Inside in warm yellow light a young woman in blinding white and a young man in deepest black were taking their vows.

I have been married for twenty-five years. I have traveled a lot but rarely alone. I always traveled, happily, with Wendy. She thinks my solo traveling is fine if quixotic. She worries. "Come back," she said when I left.

I am getting used to being alone. I rather like it.

SPANISH LESSON

A man from Venezuela who lives in New Hampshire bums a cigarette while we wait for our suitcases in the Buenos Aires airport. I don't know why, but the idea of a Venezuelan sitting before a woodburning stove in the White Mountains strikes me as odd. Then again Peter Matthiessen wrote in *The Cloud Forest* that he felt homesick when he lay down in a field in southern Chile because it reminded him of New England pastures.

I spend the afternoon with José Alberto Marchi, a painter. He takes me to his gallery in Recoleta, introduces me to the manager, a woman on crutches. "*Hola. Es un gusto*," she says and kisses my cheek. "This is the best gallery in Buenos Aires." We look at one of José's works, a small canvas called *The Raising of the Dawn*. Painted with Rembrandt-like meticulousness, it has a modern, almost conceptual twist.

We walk through the city, stopping first at the lush Plaza San Martin across from the Plaza Hotel. The plaza is studded with trees: huge palms and *jacarandas* full of fluttering blue flowers and the funny *palos borrachos* trees with their pink blossoms and sinuous trunks shaped like bottles. "The drunk trees," José says. The spacious plaza teems with life. Children crowd a sun-dappled playground, mothers and grandmothers hover nearby. An energetic soccer game is in progress. Benches are full of people reading, chatting, caressing, idling.

A while later we are standing in the Galerias Pacifico staring up at a mural — a huge collaborative work painted in the forties by a group of Argentine artists. Formerly a turn-of-the-century railroad office, the building is now a glitzy mall, an unlikely setting for the powerful social realist paintings spanning the large dome.

After a look at Plaza de Mayo, we pass by the obelisk on the Avenida 9 de Julio, the "widest street in the world." It's a warm day, a late summer day in March. We stop in a café on the Avenida Corrientes. Buenos Aires is wonderful to walk in with its cafés, baroque architecture, and tree-lined avenues. I order a beer, José tea. "I don't drink," he says. "I don't drive, either. I'm a little strange, I think."

Playground, Plaza San Martin

Actually he is quite charming. He looks a little gruff with his close-cropped black hair and patchy beard. His thick accent adds to the effect, but he is reserved and exceedingly polite. He is attentive and quick to smile. Though boyish he has a certain intensity about him. He's in his late thirties, I would guess.

Over steaks and *papas fritas* in a restaurant in Recoleta, we talk shop. Though he clearly loves painting in the style of the Old Masters, he is a little embarrassed by it. "I think I should be more modern." Still he refers frequently to older artists and has a strong sense of tradition. "He is a master," he says about one painter. "One of Argentina's most important artists."

José gives me a Spanish lesson. He explains the difference between the two forms of the verb to be: *ser* and *estar*. *Ser* is used when you refer to what you are, *estar* when you refer to where you are. He writes in my notebook: *Soy un pintor.* I am a painter. *Estoy en Buenos Aires.* I am in Buenos Aires.

CAFE TORTONI

Plaza de Mayo, the city's main square. *Mayo* was the month of independence, the year was 1810. Children chase pigeons in the warm sun on their way from the cathedral with the tomb of the liberator San Martin at one end of the plaza to the big *Casa Rosada*, the president's house, at the other end. The cathedral is fronted by forbidding classical columns. We have the White House, the Argentinians the Pink House. Painted in blood, it is said. Here, outside the *Casa Rosada*, is where mothers hold vigil for missing children. Every Thursday they come in their white scarves. Today is Saturday and the square is quiet.

I walk down Avenida de Mayo to Café Tortoni. Dark wood, red leather chairs, marble tables, paintings, pool tables, skylights. The word "literary" seems to hang in the air. Or rather *La Peña* (The Circle), the name given to avant-garde intellectuals who used to animate its tables.

I order a sandwich and a *chopp*. Two men throw dice across a table, someone hums loudly in the kitchen. A fashionable young couple comes in followed by an old man with a cane. You can tell the regulars by the way they enter and claim a table. It's six o'clock. The place starts to fill. I eat and read and watch the crowd. Though I sit alone and say little, I am revived. I feel a part of the world, of Buenos Aires. Café Tortoni, like all good cafés, combats more than one kind of hunger.

GUILLERMO AND TEATRO COLON

My knock is answered by a small gray-haired man wearing a pink shirt and sunglasses. It's 9:30 in the morning and the man is the set designer Guillermo de la Torre. He invites me into his elegant antique-filled apartment in Recoleta. "Have you had breakfast?" he asks. We sit at a beautifully set table in a glassed-in porch surrounded by plants. He pours coffee and serves cake made of apples and nuts. "Today I show you the theaters of Buenos Aires," he says.

We drive in his little car along the Avenida 9 de Julio to Teatro Colon. The venerable opera and ballet house, the size of a city block, is a second home to Guillermo. He has designed many productions for this famous place. He takes me on a tour of its underground workshops. Everywhere he is greeted warmly and addressed as "maestro." He introduces me as his *colega norteamericano.* I am flattered and charmed by this sweet pied piper of theater.

Thousands of costumes and shoes are labeled and neatly stored in one capacious room. A woman pulls a dress from a locker and drapes it across her forearm for me to admire. "Maria Callas wore this," Guillermo says. He runs his hand over the fabric. We talk with a man making a pair of black boots, a woman attaching a waist band to a tutu. Behind her on a rack are a dozen more, white frothy things lighter than air.

In the immense scene shop shirtless men stack long lengths of wood. We go into the subterranean rehearsal room equal in dimension to the stage above. The cavernous, windowless room is mysterious, almost eerie, the air heavy and dank. The sounds of the powerful voices that have soared around this room seem to linger in the musty stillness.

We ascend to the stage itself and look out at the dark house, at the chairs covered in velvet and at the ornate gold and burgundy boxes. I am struck by the beauty of the place, by the care it receives and the dedication of the people who work here. Meeting Guillermo and seeing the opera house from inside out more than makes up for the fact that it's off-season and I can't attend an opera. We have lunch in the cafeteria with a crusty but handsome comrade of Guillermo's. The man has worked at Teatro Colon as long as Guillermo. He says something and the two elderly men laugh heartily. Guillermo looks at me. "He said he hates opera."

Tutus, Teatro Colon

THE CITY OF BEAUTIFUL AIRS

"Rio de la Plata means River of Silver," José says.

We are looking at a vase made of silver in the rather grand eighteenth-century home of a man named Isaac Fernandez Blanco. It has lately become a museum for Hispanic-American art. The Spanish settled on the banks of the Rio de la Plata in the sixteenth century, thinking there was plenty of silver around. They were wrong. Their name for the river was enticing but inaccurate.

The settlement languished for a couple of hundred years (indeed the city of "beautiful airs" was thick with rats and disease for a long time) before, thanks to smuggling, it became a thriving port. There was silver in nearby Bolivia, and eventually craftsmen in Buenos Aires began to make beautiful objects like the vase José and I are admiring. Outside the house is a garden choked with flowers and trees heavy with oranges. We sit for awhile on a blue-tiled bench between two urns. "Why don't you come for dinner," José says.

A few hours later, I am standing in his kitchen. José introduces me to Claudia, his wife. She has short brown hair and a winsome way. Modest rather than shy, she has a warm smile. "She is afraid to speak English," José says. Despite the language barrier, she makes me feel welcome. We walk through their lovingly renovated apartment which fronts a busy street in the center of the city. Their two children are not at home. Jose's small neat studio in the back of the apartment feels like a monk's cell. After pouring drinks, José shows me his vast CD collection. "I love ambient music."

We are joined by Sylvia, Claudia's older and bolder sister, Alberto, an architect, and his wife, Sandra, and Tony, a decorator and designer. Alberto, a bright, talkative man with a moustache, shares José's passion for new music and the two of them listen to some discs. Tony is shy but dashing in a brilliant blue shirt.

The meal is a feast of tarts and fish and beef. Wine flows and the long table grows raucous with jokes and stories in Spanish and English. This is a good-natured crowd, not given to solemn pontification. The entertaining Alberto interrupts the banter from time to time to mock a political figure or tell a joke. They seem not too interested in

North American life. "We know what goes on," Alberto says. "We are affected by the U.S. economy and culture, but we are more drawn to European ideas and style."

In the sitting room we open the windows for fresh air. The noise of the ceaseless traffic rushes in, almost deafening even at midnight. Claudia returns from the kitchen distraught. Her desserts have failed her.

"Just call Freddo's," Tony says.

"What's Freddo's?" I ask.

"The best ice cream in the city," Sylvia says. "Everybody loves Freddo's."

"Do they deliver?"

"Yes."

"Now? It's one in the morning."

"Of course." An hour later we are back at the table spooning up Freddo's by candlelight and drinking champagne.

THE CRAZY YEARS

A mother and two daughters walk down the stone path past evergreen trees. I follow them. They turn down one of the rows of crypts. One girl is carrying flowers. The crowded rows intersect like the lanes of a village. Made of marble and stone, many of the crypts are elaborately designed small buildings. Some have morose religious tableaux, others are overrun with flowers, moss, and crumbling statuary.

This village of the dead, or more accurately, this village of the rich and famous dead is in the heart of Recoleta, the most fashionable district in Buenos Aires. Birds sing in the morning sun, old workers drag hoses and mumble among themselves. There is the sound of distant traffic.

After several wrong turns, the family stops, and the girl places the flowers on the ground before a simple black marble grave. I walk up behind them. It is the grave of Eva Peron. The woman touches the grave. She reads outloud the inscription: "*Volveré y seré millones.*" The woman looks at me. She bends down to talk to her children.

I find out later what it means. "I will come back and become millions."

I have dinner at *Los Años Locos* with Gustavo, a friend of Miroslav Kubes, the architect I met in Quito. Gustavo is an engineer who works for a company that makes pipelines. He travels the world. "The name of the restaurant means The Crazy Years," he says. He is a small man with a big chest and a strong voice.

The restaurant is one of a number of steak houses that line a section of the riverfront. Called *parrilladas,* they began as simple carts grilling meat for dock workers. Inside the front door, cooks poke forks into slabs of beef hanging above a huge open fire. Every table in the two large rooms is full. Gustavo orders for both of us: *bife de chorizo,* which, living up to billing, is delicious. "A *porteño,*" he says, pouring wine, "is someone who is Italian who speaks Spanish and wants to be English."

"And eats beef."

He talks about runaway inflation and the necessity of tolerating corrupt leaders if they straighten out the economy. "As long as they are not too corrupt."

"What about Peron?"

"Peron was Peron. He did some good things and some bad things."

"What was it like during the time of the generals?"

"Most people did not know how bad it was. The number of people who were tortured or killed."

"They know now, don't they? Do people want to hold the generals accountable?"

"Mostly they want to forget about it."

After dinner, we go to Freddo's. We sit at a table outside in the warm night, eating ice cream and telling stories like a couple of high-school kids. Ice cream and the past have something in common. They both melt. But the past has a way of coming back.

TO EAT THE WORLD

Josefina Robirosa's flat is in San Telmo. She lives on the fourth *piso* of an old French-style building with a wooden elevator and a view of a park. She comes to the door in jeans and red socks. "Would you like some tea?" she asks. We sit on her sofa beneath a ceiling fan and talk, like people freed from a cell or from a deserted island.

Josefina is a painter. She is tall, attractive, well-bred, and has, like many *porteños*, a gift for conversation. We talk for hours about everything, art, politics, families, Argentina, the pains and pleasures of life. "My generation failed," she says, "because it was full of spoiled children who all had nannies and never saw their parents. Like the English." She closes the window against the mosquitoes, pours me a glass of whiskey.

"We have always looked outside ourselves, looked to others for help, blamed others. Decadence and corruption didn't begin with Peron. Argentina used to be rich, but now, now...we have never really faced up to reality. My ideal is to have responsible, ethical people, each person responsible for his own block. Nothing more than that. Just his own block."

Josefina lives alone in her rambling apartment. We look at her landscape paintings in her studio. Sometime near midnight, we go to dinner. We walk by a square where a crowd has gathered around a couple dancing the tango. The woman sings a mournful ballad. Everyone, including Josefina, joins in with great passion, as if singing the national anthem.

"There is too much perfection in your society," she says after we sit down in a restaurant. "I had a show in Houston once and I went to a cocktail party given by the Mellons. There were exactly twenty-four oranges on each tree. And there is too much to choose from in America. You go crazy. I am trying to simplify my life. I am sixty-two and happy for the first time. I love Buenos Aires and my friends, but I only need myself. You have to be good company for yourself. You have to find meaning within yourself. Through reflection, reading. I am not so rational now. I am more content. Since my husband died, I have begun to believe in God again."

"You want calm, I want adventure."

"What kind of adventure?"

"I don't mean climbing a mountain or jumping out of an airplane. Sitting here talking to you is an adventure."

Josefina laughs. I feel slightly ridiculous, spewing pap like a character in James or Chekhov. Chatwin said Buenos Aires reminded him of Tsarist Russia, of *The Cherry Orchard*. "You are still young," she says. "You have to accomplish things. You have to go around the world."

"I don't feel young. I feel mortal. I want to embrace the world, to eat the world."

"I don't think it's on the menu."

We take a taxi back to Josefina's apartment and I say goodbye. It's three a.m. The lights of the avenue are bright, the sidewalks noisy with people. The city is very much alive. I tumble into bed in this feverish place at the end of the world, exhausted, exhilarated, talked out, and slightly drunk.

Manzanas, San Telmo

STEREOTYPE

"Everybody in Argentina has a soccer ball in his head," José says as the bus passes the stadium, *La Bombonera*, or Box of Candy. José and I, along with Claudia and Sylvia, are headed to La Boca, the working-class district at "the mouth" of the river on the city's south side. Italian sailors and others who worked on the river settled here in the nineteenth century. They lived in houses made of corrugated metal scavenged from old ships. Many of the houses, painted in brilliant primary colors, have survived.

A few tourists this Sunday drift through the streets. Cantinas and dance halls and tango dancers in the street add to the local color. On El Caminito, a man on a stool squeezes the *bandoneon*. He seems bored to tears. Next to him a woman in long curly hair belts out a song. José seems half-pained, half-amused by the canned atmosphere. I heard Astor Piazzola perform several years ago. I love his nuevo tango, and I think I would like the traditional stuff, too, if I could get beyond the stereotype. When I ask José what he thinks of tango, he makes a face. We stop at the port where stranded fishing boats tilt in the mud. The stench of the brown river drives us away. We walk through the neighborhood. Tall daisies grow along a railroad track, lines of clothes dry in the sun. Boys kick a soccer ball against a graffiti-smeared wall, skinny dogs roam.

In San Telmo, on Plaza Dorrego, antique dealers have spread their wares on tables. Cafés and shops are open, people crowd around dancers. We browse in the hot sun. Sylvia bargains with one of the vendors. I look at *maté* gourds and the metal straws called *bombillas*. Many of the gourds and straws are made of silver and are quite ornate. I think of gauchos in old photos sipping *maté* on the pampas. Tango, *maté*, gaucho. I have traveled thousands of miles to see Buenos Aires for myself, to bust the stereotype, to cast off stale images planted in my head by movies, newspapers, television.

On the Avenida Corrientes, we find a table at a popular pizza place. We joke and laugh, talk about life in the U.S. It's hard to say goodbye. I hug Claudia. She looks at me, screwing up her courage to speak. "You are very nice," she says in English.

"*Eres muy simpática*," I say.

Sugarloaf Mountain

RIVER OF JANUARY

Downtown Rio is pretty dismal. Most of the buildings are modern and uninteresting (Brazilians, like North Americans, have a passion for tearing things down), but the neoclassical museum, library, and theater along Avenida Rio Branco, the city's main drag, have age and weight and form a sort of center in the chaos of people and whirling traffic. The wide Frenchlike boulevard used to be lined with turn of the century neoclassical buildings.

A few blocks away, full of trees and vendors, is Rio's oldest square, called Praça XV after the day — November 15, 1889 — Brazil became a republic. On the square is the sprawling eighteenth-century imperial palace with a courtyard and thick stone walls. The palace, also the city post office for a while, has been restored and is now a cultural center.

Heavy rain falls on the creaking baroque churches and faded colonial buildings. Across from the Candelaria Church are school children at an exhibition in what was once a bank. Among the displays is a metal box, like a paint box, containing human hair. Strands of hair are tied in bunches. They vary in color from the red of brick to the yellow of cornsilk to the black of crow's wing. There are thirty shades in all. Some strands are kinky, some straight, some wavy. Also on display are thirty-six painted swatches of skin color and eyes painted in sixteen colors. Not a bad way to show the broad mix of Brazil's people, and of the world's.

A Swiss woman who runs a small restaurant in an arcade near the palace tells me about places she likes in the neighborhood. One of them is the seventeenth-century Sao Bento Monastery farther north along the bay. The monastery is on a hill an elevator ride from a shop on the street below. Monks in robes walk the grounds inured to the wonderful view. Inside the chapel is endless gold leaf on wood. By the bay is a navy base with off duty sailors milling around. Their white caps have *Marinha do*

 *Brasil* printed on the black trim. One of the shops across the street sells military gear. The classic cap is made of plastic.

In a bookstore near the old palace is a book with old photos of Rio. Rio's near pristine setting in the hundred-year-old pictures must be close to what Amerigo Vespucci saw when he first came upon it in 1502. It was in the month of January. He thought he had discovered a river, which is how the River of January got its name. Curious how the mistakes of explorers become fixed in time. What he really found was a big bay. The Indians called it *Guanabara* (Arm of the Sea).

After poking around the tacky Cindelândia area, I take a taxi back to the hotel. We drive by the bay past the swooping mythical beaches. When we pass the Copacabana Palace, the driver points to the moldy but still glamorous looking spread and says "Princess Diana."

DREAMERS

I'm lost. I'm standing outside a large brick building on a street in a rundown section of Rio. It's nine in the morning. A woman, the only other person around, turns out to be the assistant of Marcio Calvão, the man I am to meet. She leads me to his office. "*Bom dia*," says a small handsome man. "Coffee?"

Marcio is executive director of the Fundição Progresso, a turn of the century foundry that is being transformed into a cultural and commercial center. He is a civil engineer by training and a one-time actor. He's about forty. In fast and furious Portuguese, Marcio tells me about his project. His elegant assistant translates.

"The building will be mixed," he says. "Culture and shopping. Theaters, galleries, cinemas, restaurants, shops. We open the first stage in the fall." He tells me about other buildings he has restored in Brazil and about his visit to U.S. cities to study preservation. An intense man, he draws and makes notes as he talks and pulls at his trim beard. He is determined to bring life back to the inner city.

"I am happy to know you care about the city, too," he says. When I ask if we are romantic dreamers, he pulls out a thick marketing plan and says, "I have a vision, an intellectual concept, but my feet are on the earth." He taps the plan.

"Do you think cities are dying?"

"We must fight to save them," he says, his voice rising. "I will show you the building."

The big theater has a long way to go, but the rest of the building is mostly finished. I like the soaring heights and the flowing way the spaces connect. Marcio takes me up to the second level, to the restaurants. We walk out on a large terrace.

"People in the restaurants can look out at the *arcos*," he says. He points to the colonnade of white arches supporting the aqueduct that runs next to the building. Built in the eighteenth century, it now carries trolley cars instead of water. A yellow trolley comes toward us. It seems to emerge from a church at the top of the hill. Palm trees are silhouetted against the sky behind the church. "Beautiful, no?" Marcio says in English.

"Beautiful, yes."

EYE CANDY

Rio is eye candy, a place set in such extraordinary natural beauty, it's no wonder *cariocas* are hedonists. One of the world's great pleasures must be to stand at the top of Corcovado as the sun sets. The view is 360 degrees, but the main action is east and north, as the gentle hills enveloping the bay grow dark in the waning light. The purple hills seem soft as cats.

Sugarloaf Mountain juts up perfectly, centering the masterpiece. The hard city turns into something miraculous. The city's lights pulse in the darkening sky and the ugly skyscrapers become brushstrokes. Slums glow like ornaments. Even an airplane landing seems dropped from the hand of God. You don't know whether the 700-ton Christ behind you with arms spread wide is calling you back from this glorious beauty or offering it to you.

THE ART OF DRINKING IN RIO

"I can't live without a view," Paolo says. "Do you have a view in Minneapolis?" We are sitting in a tiny restaurant in Leblon owned by Paolo's sister. We are drinking *caipirinhas* with passion fruit. Paolo has an athlete's build. He's wearing jeans and a white T-shirt that shows off his Brazilian color. He just spent four months traveling in Asia and is now back at his job as a chef in a restaurant south of Rio.

"I've been married twice," he says. "Well, I lived several years with one woman then with another and that means I was married in Brazil. Legally married even though we never got married in a church." He orders another round of drinks.

Paolo is showing me the art of drinking in Rio. "First we eat black beans with nuts and parsley to line the palate for the *cachaça*," he says. *Cachaça* is the high proof alcohol made from sugar cane used to make a *caipirinha*. Like grain alcohol, it packs a wallop. The restaurant specializes in food from northern Brazil. Small portions of crab with manioc and beef with pumpkin sauce are brought to the table. I wish there were more food. My head is pounding.

Friends of Paolo's join us, a thin man with a beatnik goatee and his girlfriend. She gives me a *beijo* on both cheeks. The man says he studied at UCLA in the sixties. "It was wild." They talk about *Pulp Fiction* which has just arrived in Rio. "An incredible movie," the woman says. "Is it really like that in the U.S.? So violent?"

I ask about crime in Rio. "Stay in the neighborhoods in the city," Paolo says. "The poor are in the suburbs. You don't have to worry. Robbers go after the old people."

"People run here even more than in the U.S."

"*Cariocas* are obsessed with their bodies," Paolo says.

We talk a little about politics. "The president is an intellectual," Paolo says.

"He is not a corrupt dictator," his friend says, a little defensively.

We talk about language. "Do you have any sense of connection to Portugal?" I ask.

"No," Paolo says. "We speak the same language, but that's it."

"We think the Portuguese are...," the woman says. "How do you say?" She tilts her head back and pushes up the tip of her nose with a forefinger.

IPANEMA

The view of Ipanema Beach from my eleventh floor window is uninspiring. The beach is straight and not especially pretty. Small waves spread across the wide stretch of sand. A single oil well breaks the flat horizon of gray sea. A light rain falls on and off. Wind rattles my window and tosses the branches of the palm trees. Traffic speeds down the four-lane road next to the beach.

Some people are walking dogs, others are running along the wide patterned sidewalk. A group of women is doing aerobic exercises. Two-person coed volleyball teams set up high tech nets and, after much stretching, leap valiantly after the ball, as if it were the Olympics. The rain turns to mist. In the hotel dining room on the second floor, I sit at a table next to the window. Breakfast is café con leche, tiny stale croissants, and mango. I continue to watch the life on the beach.

Away from the tall apartments and hotels, Ipanema has the pleasant intimate feel of a village with its streets of trees, shops, and cafés. In a grocery store are stacks of salt cod folded like blankets, great quantities of black beans, rice, and *limons*. There are eggplants, long green beans, okra. Only men work at the checkout registers.

On the sidewalk along the beach red signs warn of polluted water. New streetlights were installed, I read, because the beach was becoming too dangerous at night. I stop at one of the *suco* stands and buy a fruit drink.

"*Obrigado*," I say to the young vendor.

He smiles and says, "Thank you. Ciao."

I notice a couple I saw in the grocery store waving at a man sitting alone on a blanket in the sand. They sit down with him and pull food from a basket. A Brazilian at the American Embassy told me that Rio is a city of neighborhoods. "The beach is where everyone meets." In Rio the square is the beach.

Beach, Ipanema

PELOURINHO

The city of Salvador sits on cliffs above a huge bay about seven hundred miles up the coast from Rio. Salvador is the capitol of the province of Bahia. Though north, it's warmer than Rio. It's closer to the equator. Traveling north to warmth seems strange to a North American. Leaving the airport terminal, I walk straight outdoors. There are no doors or windows. The taxi passes under arching bamboo trees.

From my room at the hotel, I can hear the sea and the beating of drums. Small black and white birds dart among the palm trees on the beach. Salvador casts a spell, people say. I gaze out the open window at dark blue water. I feel a breeze and the pull of the tropics.

I head straightaway to Pelourinho, the old part of town, past the bus station and city hall on the Praça da Se in the Cidade Alta, or upper city. In the plaza of Terreiro de Jesus, a man in dreadlocks named Wellington buttonholes me. He is all smiles and fast talk. "You want to go to *candomble*? Are you German, English?"

Pelourinho Square is dominated by the sunny blue *casa* of Jorge Amado. The house is filled with photographs of the celebrated writer with famous European writers and actors. The book jackets of his many books, including *Dona Flor and Her Two Husbands*, are on display. In colonial days it was not literature but slaves and criminals that were on display around here. The pillory, the primitive jail with holes for an offender's head and hands, was so commonplace it gave the neighborhood its name. Pelourinho means pillory.

The first thing you notice is color. Many of the old buildings have been freshly painted in eye-popping pastels. Much of Pelourinho's colonial architecture is intact (it is said to be the most stunning in the New World), and the city, with one eye on the tourist, is fixing up its treasures. At moments the place seems almost too pretty, the paint almost too fresh, even for one who loves the picturesque. The pink, yellow, and blue façades provide lovely backdrop. *Baianos* lean in doorways, look down from balconies, sit in café windows.

It feels good to walk in an old center that has not been destroyed, that still has a soul. On the cobbled hilly streets are more people than cars. Shops sell colorful souvenir paintings, leather goods, and postcards. But doors also open on to seamstresses, printers, and greengrocers. Music floats on the warm soft air. The atmosphere is relaxed, sensual. But there is a slight edge to it. I can't put my finger on it. Children look a little too ragamuffin. Skinny teenage boys roam around. Lots of men seem idle. Policemen stand on corners. You can't paint over poverty. But it's not just that. There is something else in the air, some unnamable energy. Maybe it comes from the pervasive Bahian mysticism, from *candomblé*, from all that spilled chicken blood. Maybe it comes from *carnaval*.

Following pages: *Pelourinho*

AT DADA'S

I have dinner with Fernanda and Vladimir, friends of people I know in Minneapolis. We go to a place called Dada's. "There is a *favela* next to the restaurant," Vladimir says. Vladimir works for the city helping small businesses. He is Slavic, low-key and down to earth. Red-haired Fernanda is Brazilian, teaches English, and has a gift shop. She is energetic and voluble. A woman in native garb comes to our outdoor table.

"David, this is Dada. She is the cook," Fernanda says. "She is famous for her Bahian dishes." Dada tells us what to eat. There is music in the background, American and Bahian. We eat marinated octopus and shrimp in manioc. We drink *caipirinhas* then big bottles of Brahma beer served in Styrofoam coolers. Fernanda and Vladimir like to talk. The conversation goes well into the night.

Fernanda: "I am from Fortaleza, two thousand kilometers north of here. São Paolo is two thousand kilometers to the south. It takes four days to drive on bad roads."

Vladimir: "My mother is Russian. My father is from Yugoslavia."

Fernanda: "Salvador has personality. It has kept its traditions."

Vladimir: "Rio and São Paolo are big cities. They have money and culture, but they are like any big city. And they are dangerous."

Fernanda: "Salvador has one church for every day of the year."

Vladimir: "The population of Salvador is growing sixteen percent a year. The World Health Organization says three to four percent is bad. The church won't allow birth control. People have many children. They think they will work and take care of them."

Fernanda: "Salvador is laid back. People are lazy. There is no stress."

Vladimir: "Politicians talk, but no real work is done."

Fernanda: "*Carnaval* in Rio, you watch. In Salvador, you participate. You can't help but dance. Everything closes down for a week. People spend four hundred dollars on a costume. They join a block and wear the costume of that block. They follow a truck decorated like a float that has music blaring from speakers inside."

Vladimir: "*Favela* mean invasion."

Fernanda: "Is it really as violent in America as we think it is?"

PAST AND PRESENT

The fountain on the Terreiro de Jesus is surrounded by trees and churches. I linger by the fountain for awhile then cross a smaller square and go into the Igreja de San Francisco. The baroque interior overwhelms, all carved wood thickly layered in gold. Is excessive gold proof of profound faith? It's too much, too cloying. But the church is bathed in natural light. The soft luminous glow, and the hush, create a feeling of transcendence. To me light is god. Outside a smiling woman with round shoulders calls to me from the door of a shop. "Would you like to have a drink?"

Crowds of men loiter in front of city hall and the bus station on the Praça Municipal. A big blue open air elevator drops down to the lower city, Cidade Baixa. Here is the commercial center of old Salvador, colonial still but neglected and crumbling. Here is the hustle and bustle of the real world, of the twentieth century. Is this more real than the touristy, gussied up historic center in the upper city? Probably. There are banks and businessmen talking earnestly and women sorting through racks of cheap clothes. This is familiar and satisfying but aesthetically less pleasing. Can't the two exist together: the rawness of the present and the charm of the past? Or must they be separate — the upper city and the lower city?

Two men run strips of sugar cane through a primitive press that extracts the juice for *cachaça*. Nearby an old man sells apples from a huge sack sitting on a curb. Mercado Modelo is a round building made of concrete where Bahian handicrafts are sold. White-haired British tourists pore over pretty cotton fabrics and other souvenirs. Outside *baianos* sit at tables and drink from big bottles of beer. Several boys wave necklaces.

Across the street boys are diving from a wall into the bay. A couple of them begin to fight with their feet. They take turns swirling and kicking, their heels coming within inches of the other's face. They see me watching and pose while I take pictures. "*Capoeira*," one of them says. When I turn to walk away, the boy steps in front of me and holds out his hand. "Contribution," he says in a tough guy voice.

THE FRUITS OF BAHIA

Silvia is Fernanda's sister. She is dark-haired and talkative like Fernanda. On our way to the market, we stop at a hut on the beach where a man whacks a coconut with a machete and pours liquid into a glass for me. The market is in Rio Vermelho, one of Salvador's better neighborhoods. "I do not go to the central market," Silvia says. "It's too dirty."

Along with fruits and vegetables, beautifully displayed in stalls marked by brightly painted signs, there are flowers, birds, and items for *candomblé*. Silvia stops at her regular vendors, talks and laughs with them. "I buy twenty pounds of beans and rice a month. I have three live-in staff. They eat a lot." She tells me the names of fruit I've never seen and puts them in her basket. "We will have them for lunch."

We pass a security guard as we enter her suburban neighborhood. The house is spacious and modern. Light floods the living room through large windows. Big abstract paintings by Brazilian artists hang on the walls. Outside there is a pool surrounded by tropical flowers and trees of avocados, mangos, and bananas. *Caipirinhas* in hand, we walk in the garden.

"There is a Portuguese saying," Silvia says. "If you build a house, plant a tree, and have a child, then you can write a book. I've done all three, including designing this house. Now maybe I will write a book."

We go inside to her husband's air-conditioned study. "Paolo is in the cocoa business," she says. A uniformed maid brings us crisp manioc. Fruffy, the dog, comes in followed by Silvia's teenaged daughter and son. We are joined at the buffet lunch by Fernanda. We sit, children included, at a long formal table and eat a kind of quiche of chicken and bacon prepared by the cook.

"You must come back and visit our house on Itaparica," Silvia says. "It's a beautiful island just across the bay. Paolo commutes to work by boat."

Her daughter talks about her experience as an exchange student in the U.S. "The people I stayed with were not very nice."

"Mussolini and Hitler," her brother says.

In a basket on the table is the fruit from the market. Silvia places them one by one on my plate. The others abstain choosing instead to watch me. "This is *caqui*," Silvia says. "It looks a little like a tomato. You eat it with a spoon."

"It's sweet," I say, feeling self-conscious. I draw each fruit in my notebook: the custard-like *pinha,* the big, green, rough skinned jackfruit, or *jaca,* the orange yellow *cirigüela,* a plum that you eat whole, and the *umbu,* another plum that you bite into and suck. It tastes like an orange.

Fernanda says something in Portuguese to Silvia then translates for me. "I remember another American who visited us. All he wanted was meat and potatoes."

GIFT

I hear drums and a man singing as I enter the shop. "Whose music is playing?" I ask the young man behind the counter.

"Gilberto Gil." He hands me a CD. "One of the best from Bahia." I ask about other music from Bahia. He puts on another CD. Loud horns and drums burst through the speakers. "Olodum," he says. "You know Olodum? They play with Paul Simon." The young man has long, thin fingers. We listen for awhile then he slips another disc into the player. "Also very good, very well-known." We listen for a few moments to the mellow voice of Caetano Veloso. "Wait," he says.

He disappears into a back room, comes out with a disc. He hands the box to me. "Toquinho," he says. "My favorite." We listen to a man playing acoustic guitar and singing a plaintive ballad. "Simple," the young man says.

"Melancholy," I say. He looks at me, not understanding. "Melancholy, sad."

"Yes, sad," he says. "Like me." He laughs.

I pick up a smooth rock lying on the counter.

"From the sea," he says. "I give it to you."

Outside the shop a *baina* sells *acarajé* and fried sweets. She is wearing the traditional big skirt and a scarf wrapped around her head. She waves her big palm across her table of food. I feel a little unfriendly when I say no. I smile, she smiles back.

After lunch with Fernanda and Vladimir, we go to their apartment. It's a small place with a view of the ocean. We pass by their children's school, rather crudely built of cement. They have three children, Isabel, Peter, and Ismini. I am introduced to shy Isabel. She shows me her drawings. We sit in the living room. A maid brings soft drinks. Fernanda tells me they adopted Ismini.

"Mini was the daughter of Vlado's sister," she says. "His sister died of an aneurysm. She was married to an older Greek man. She spoke eight languages. We had a boy named John who died in utero at term two months after Mini was born." This comes without warning. But Fernanda speaks about it in a straightforward way with little emotion in her voice.

She gives me a piece of lace for Wendy. She puts it in a small bag painted by her mother. "Write us," Vladimir says as we say goodbye. Fernanda gives me a big hug. "You must come back," she says.

Baina

SOMEONE ELSE

The taxi takes the beach road north to the airport. It's early evening. The streets fill with the sweet-natured people of this enchanting, needy city. We pass long lines of people waiting for buses, small wooden kiosks selling fruit, and shops with meat hanging from hooks. On one corner, a woman with a high round forehead pulls her ebony hair back and clamps it in place with a barrette. She smiles at a man watching her. Boys play soccer on the beaches. Men sit on stools at the huts that line the beach.

Cool evening air rushes in the window. The driver names each beach as we pass. "*Aqui Piata Praia. Aqui Itapua Praia.*" The beaches are as alluring as their names. He says each name two or three times, then pauses, waiting for me to say it. He speaks with great pride. His Portuguese is a mixture of harshness and singsong.

My flight to São Paolo has been cancelled. I rush to the gate of another flight, join the crush of people. It's a long trip home. A strange feeling comes over me when I hand the immigration man in Miami my passport. It is not my passport. It is my name and my photograph, but it is not my passport.

It is the passport of someone else.

THE END OF RESTLESSNESS

BARCELONA — Favorite Square / Tapas and Talk / Heart of Stone / The Real City / Tears / Gaudí's Bed / New China on an Old Table / Streets / Is This Our Lot? / The Spanish Painter — 100

PRAGUE — Wedding Cake / City of Music / Malá Strana / Alchemy / The World's Most Beautiful Amusement Park / The First to Die / Dinner with Vladimir / Bridge — 123

STOCKHOLM — Same Old Way / Summer Place / Stortorget / City of Water / The Opera Singer / The End of Restlessness / The Golden Peace — 141

BERLIN — The Place to Be / Berlin without the Wall / Western Style / A City with a River / Sunday in the Park / Topography of Terror / Ilka / A Religious Experience / Kaiser — 153

Plaça Reial

BARCELONA

FAVORITE SQUARE

"It's a good time to be in Barcelona," Stephen says. "In August everyone wilts." It is a late afternoon in early July. The sun is shining, there is a breeze. We sit outside drinking a sweet, milky drink made with nuts. The café is in Eixample across the street from the gallery where Stephen and José Ramon work. The gallery had once been a hatter's shop (there is a hat above the door of the gallery), the shop owner a patron of the arts, of Miró in particular. "Calder decorated the windows for the shop one year," José Ramon says. "He made a mobile of hats."

    The gallery is on the same block as Antoni Gaudí's Casa Batlló. Also on the block are the exuberant buildings of Lluís Domènech i Montaner and Josep Puig i Cadafalch, Gaudí's fellow *modernistas*. My guidebook calls the ensemble of competing styles *"manzana de la discòrdia"* ("block of discord"), but Jose Ramon refers to it as the "golden square."

    Stephen invites me to an opening in a gallery in the Gothic quarter. We walk beneath the plane trees of the Ramblas past kiosks, flower vendors, Croatian street performers, couples drinking wine. "This doesn't exist anywhere else in Europe," Stephen says. "Las Ramblas is Arabic." We pass the Boqueria market, the bird sellers, the Miró stones. We stop for a moment in front of the beautiful but sad shell of Teatre del Liceu. The opera singer Montserrat Caballé, a Catalan, stood in tears before the opera house when it burned two years ago.

    "This is my favorite square," Stephen says as we sit down at a café in the Plaça Reial. It is beautiful if a little seedy. I like its size, like a football field but wider and shorter, the arcades, the uniformity of the mock-French nineteenth-century architecture, the Gaudí lamps on either side of the fountain, the palm trees, the sense of enclosure, the absence of traffic. "It used to be overrun with dope dealers."

Birds, The Ramblas

At the gallery, the artist, a lanky Canadian, shakes hands, kisses cheeks. His big expressionist paintings of comic book children surround the smart opening night crowd. Victor, a painter from Mexico City, with a sad face and a soft voice, tells me he has lived abroad for fifteen years, including time studying architecture at Harvard and Columbia. "Barcelona is provincial. It is socially impenetrable. A wonderful place to visit but not to live."

I ask him if he has seen the movie *Barcelona*.

"You mean 'WASPS Abroad?'"

TAPAS AND TALK

Stephen and I find a table outside at a restaurant on the Passeig de Gràcia. We eat tapas and talk about restlessness. Stephen says that his family was exiled from Alexandria in the fifties when Nasser kicked Jews out of Egypt. His family went first to the Continent, then to London. Stephen lived for many years on Mallorca before moving to Barcelona five years ago. He is a thoughtful man, somewhat aloof, in his early fifties. Gray curls are visible at the top of his shirt which is partly unbuttoned.

"We had to leave Alexandria in three days," he says. "My father had to sell his collection of Oriental rugs to Army officers for next to nothing. I vowed never to be under the tyranny of property, never to be attached to objects."

I talk about my itinerant childhood, about my search for place and my doubts about finding it. "I love American mobility," Stephen says. "I love places like L.A. and Venice Beach." He argues against rootedness. "When you have property you have to defend it. You always feel threatened, you are always encumbered. Property is too much worry, it costs too much, it makes people afraid. Why do we imbue places, things with special meaning? Why care about a lock of hair or a chair? It's fetishistic, sentimental, and treacherous. Better to just have the memory of them."

"People can be treacherous," I say.

"I care for people not objects," he says. "I am against the sentimental, for the romantic."

"Objects provide comfort and pleasure. A chair or a lock of hair is meaningful each time you look at it."

"It only has the meaning you give it. You have the memory of it."

"Desire for place or beauty is innately human."

"You don't need to possess just experience."

My ideal is to have both roots and freedom, attachment to place and the ability to travel. "Most people can't afford this, or don't have the opportunity," Stephen says. He says he understands American restlessness having seen the soullessness of

American cities. "I love the nature in America. A New Mexico sunset is more beautiful than a Gaudí building. America is such a huge country, there is so much nature, everyone speaks English. Why travel abroad if you haven't seen your own country?"

Looking in my notebook, I find this from Shakespeare's *As You Like It*. Rosalind says to Jacques: "A traveler! By my faith, you have great reason to be sad. I fear you have sold your own lands to see other men's; then, to have seen much and to have nothing is to have rich eyes and poor hands."

HEART OF STONE

Nuria Ruig, a young woman with hair tinted the color of a Spanish *rioja*, works for the Museum of Contemporary Art as assistant to the director. We meet at a cafe on the Passeig de Gràcia. She has a Mediterranean gregariousness and sense of fun. "You want to see the heart of the city? Come with me."

We head for the barri Gòtic, leaving modern Barcelona behind at the sprawling Plaça de Catalunya. We slip into the dark streets of the ancient Gothic quarter as if into another world. There are no cars, there is no bustle. The noise of the city vanishes. It is an extraordinary transition into a dreamy mix of small squares and shops, tiles and faded frescoes, gargoyles, fountains, and heavy wooden doors. We pass façade after façade of shuttered windows and iron balconies filled with pots of geraniums and singing birds. The colors of the stone walls are the colors of the earth: tan, ochre, gray, sienna, darkened with age. The old buildings have the spareness and severity of Gothic architecture, but they also have, in their restraint and simplicity, an emotional power, a strength.

Plaça de la Seu, the square in front of the city's dark cathedral, opens on to a walking street in front of the old-fashioned Hotel Colón. People stroll between the church and the hotel, stopping to talk or play or read the paper. It's a classic urban setting, a little stage-like with the distinguished buildings all around, but it simmers like a stew with real life. Kids kick a soccer ball, ladies with shopping bags talk earnestly, businessmen conspire.

Nuria shows me a stone mailbox carved with turtles and swallows outside the door of an old mansion. The courtyards of the old casas have entryways large enough for horses and massive outdoor stairways climbing to the sky. We walk down the Street of Paradise, under the Bridge of Sighs, and stop at the Square of the King, the stony heart of Gothic Barcelona. On the Square of the Angel, a wedding party gathers. Dressed in suits of raven's black, their hair even blacker, the young men and women smoke, preen, and look around anxiously.

"Now we go to my favorite church," Nuria says. When it was built in the fourteenth century, Santa Maria del Mar stood next to the sea. The people of the town lived by the sea and prayed by the sea, prayed to Mary, the mother of a fisherman. The interior of the church is a model of simplicity and transcendence. A semicircle of columns takes your eye to the radiant nave high above and subliminally to the heavens above that. A choir rehearses.

We emerge from the dark carrers into sunny Plaça Sant Jaume. "This is where the *adjutament* is, the government," Nuria says. She points to the town hall on one side of the plaza and to the offices for the region of Catalunya on the other. Red and yellow flags, bearing the likeness of the ubiquitous St. George, dot the immaculate square.

We walk up the Ramblas as the sun goes down. We end up in a crowded tapas bar, sitting at the counter, eating and drinking beer. "You smoke?" Nuria says. "I didn't think Americans smoked. If it makes you smile, why not? Smoking, eating, enjoying life. It's O.K., if it's done in moderation." The conversation turns to romance. "Women can be more independent today in Spain," Nuria says. "We can live on our own. We don't need to get married right away, we don't always need a man."

Under a starless sky, Nuria hikes up her skirt and climbs on her motorbike. Her home is up the mountain Tibidabo half an hour away. "My moto is better than a man." She looks at me and laughs. She kicks the little bike to life. "It's more reliable. It's always there."

THE REAL CITY

"This is the real city," Sergi Aguilar says and makes a sweeping gesture toward the buildings around us. He lights a cigarette as we walk around his sculpture on Rua Julia, a street in a working-class neighborhood. The sculpture is a tall minimalist piece in steel, reminiscent of Joel Shapiro's work. Sitting on a bench in the park nearby are Sergi's wife, Virginia, and year-old daughter, Blanca.

Sergi's sculpture and the park found life as part of a program to bring art and trees to rundown barrios. The program was started by Barcelona's socialist mayor, Pasqual Maragall, the grandson of the famous Catalan poet, Joan Maragall. (I read in Robert Hughes's *Barcelona* about the younger Maragall's idea that a world of cities might fare better than the world of nations. Nations are slow and have more language barriers, Maragall said. "Cities have no frontiers, no armies, no customs, no immigration officials. Cities are places for invention, for creativity, for freedom.")

"I like your sculpture," I tell Sergi. "Do you mind that a man is leaning on it?" Sergi is a small, soft-spoken man in his late forties with pleasing wrinkles at his eyes and short dark hair, what little is left. Virginia is a handsome, confident woman, a little taller than Sergi. Lively Blanca walks between my legs and holds my hand.

We circle the city in Barcelona's famously bad traffic. A brief stop to look at a Richard Serra sculpture of concrete curving across a playground. It has not aged well, a chronic problem of public art. More recent pieces by Ellsworth Kelly and Claes Oldenberg are impressive if familiar. All this work is in rough and tumble neighborhoods. In a cheap café, we stand with coffee before an unappetizing array of tapas.

"To the sea," Sergi announces. We drive along the port, passing the Olympic village apartments, once home to the world's athletes now to Barcelonans. Past Barceloneta's crowded beach is more American sculpture, a head by Roy Lichtenstein, a Frank Gehry fish. Nearby a statue of Columbus points out to sea (in the direction of Africa not America) from the Gate of Peace. Columbus was received by Ferdinand and Isabella in Barcelona after his first voyage to the New World.

Square with Serra Sculpture

On the road up Montjuic, we take in the view of the harbor and the sun-baked city, which spreads from the sea across a shallow valley and up hillsides. There are few tall buildings. The Sagrada Familia looms in the distance as do other church spires. To the west is Tibidabo. We arrive at the Miró Foundation in time for lunch.

Going down the mountain, we stop at the recreated pavillion designed by Mies van der Rohe for the 1929 World's Fair. Made of exquisite marble and onyx with a pool of rocks, it is a modernist's dream. A brick *modernista* building off the Passeig de Gràcia that was once a publishing house is now home of the Tàpies Foundation. The main floor is given over to temporary exhibitions. In the basement are Antoni Tàpies's paintings.

"I love Tàpies," Sergi says. "He is a Catalan. He lives in Barcelona." The large canvasses are covered with Tàpies's eloquent, painful scribbles. Most of them were painted during the Franco era. They are powerful and life-affirming. People find a way to speak even in dark times.

I call home when I get back to the hotel. My mother has taken a turn for the worse and is back in the hospital. I cannot speak to her.

TEARS

In a famous fin-de-siècle restaurant once frequented by artists, including the young Picasso (who in photographs of the time, sporting a goatee and bolo tie, seems quite the insolent dandy), I sit in a crowded painting-filled room, the only one eating alone. A man plays a piano with insouciance and weariness.

Memories of my mother. On her beloved Texas island sitting on the couch in her house with the big windows and plush carpet. She is wearing shorts, her bare feet tucked under her, smoke from a cigarette disappearing into the purifier. The television is on. She has a glass of vodka in her hand and is laughing out loud. It is late. My father has already gone to bed. She looks to see if I am laughing. She has not yet begun dialysis.

My father and brothers tell me that I don't need to return to Texas. Mom's situation is bad but not catastrophic. The waiter pours the last of the wine. Outside, I am quickly and gladly lost in the moody streets of a foreign city. I walk for hours. On the Ramblas, a drunk prostitute with a cast on her arm falls in beside me. "English? French?" I keep walking. She stays with me. "Give me a cigarette." I pull one from my pocket. "Thank you. Love? *L'amour?*"

No, I have love. It's something else, I'm not sure what. Farther up the Ramblas, nearly deserted at this hour, I see a young American with a bloody mouth. He is screaming profanities at somebody. He walks quickly, looking over his shoulder. He may be screaming at another man, I can't tell.

I cross Plaça de Catalunya. I look up at the clock on the tower. Four a.m. I am exhausted. Tears for my mother. For myself, too, I suppose, and for the prostitute and the guy with the bloody mouth. Tears for the something that was lost, or perhaps was never there.

GAUDI'S BED

Antoni Gaudí's Casa Milà is a massive complex of apartments made of undulating blue gray stone. Nicknamed snidely *La Pedrera*, or The Quarry, it was built around the turn of the century. Freeform grotesque iron balconies cling to the walls like insects. There is not a single straight line in the building. It is all organic waves and curves. "The straight line is an invention," Gaudí said. "It does not exist in nature."

The interior is closed for renovation, but the roof is open. Up six flights of stairs are the famous chimneys. The surfaces of these large spiral mushroom-like structures are covered with broken ceramic tiles and other found objects. Pieces of champagne bottles are stuck to one. Arabic women, Turkish architecture, a drug-induced fantasy: Gaudí's Casa Milà chimneys have been called all these things.

The Sagrada Familia is even more fantastical. Walking to it from the metro station in the hot midday sun is like approaching a mirage. Is it real? The soaring spires and reptilian skin inspire awe and give you the creeps at the same time. Unfinished and unsuccessful, this is Gaudí's most famous work. It is at once tragic and kitschy, sublime and ridiculous. The church is remarkable more for the vision, the fanaticism of its creator than for its splendor. Gaudí in old age was obsessed with finishing this lyrical monster. He lived in a hut on the grounds of the Sagrada Familia at the time of his death in 1920. Celebrated but poor, he died after being hit by a tram.

Parc Güell is perhaps the most enchanting spot in Gaudí's world. The former estate of Gaudí's patron, Eusebi Güell, it has the feeling of an amusement park. At the entrance are two Gaudí pavilions, whimsical despite the heavy stonework, and a giant tiled lizard fountain. Behind the fountain is an open room of columns supporting a white ceiling decorated with circles of colored tile. The ceiling turns out to be the floor of a large open courtyard above. Around the sandy courtyard is a long serpentine bench. It curves and winds for over a hundred meters. The bench is made of thousands of pieces of brilliantly patterned broken tile, placed in seemingly random patterns. People sit reading, sunbathing, looking out at Barcelona.

The bench was designed not by Gaudí but by one of his asssistants. It is a marvelous thing, far more effective as public art than the city's more serious sculpture. Public art or public decoration, when it works, is powerful precisely because it is public, because it is enjoyed with others. Like going to the movies.

On the grounds is the lovely pink house where the architect lived for twenty years. A path winds through stone grottoes and lavish gardens to the house. The house, now a museum, is filled with examples of Gaudí's seductive Art Nouveau furniture and some of his possessions. In one room are a typewriter and his bed. The bed is small and plain. A bed whether slept in by Gaudí or by an anonymous gardener is a thing of supreme pathos. An empty bed recalls more vividly than almost any other material object the existence, the life of another human being. It is most poignantly telling of our vulnerability, our need for shelter, for home.

La Sagrada Família

NEW CHINA ON AN OLD TABLE

The new Museum of Contemporary Art is so white and glistening it looks like a piece of fine china set down on the worn brown table that is Barcelona's Raval quarter. It is just to the west of the Ramblas. Raval means slum though as I walk through it on my way to the museum I don't think of it as a slum. Richard Meier's dazzling museum is obviously a feather in the city's cap, but the museum seems out of place. Talk about context. It's so white, and everything around it is so much of the earth, so much of a neighborhood.

Inside, Antonia Maria Perelles, the museum's head curator, is wringing her hands. An appealing woman from Mallorca, and Nuria's boss, she tells me the new museum's curved walls are going to be difficult to hang art on. The museum may have to build another set of straight, mobile walls within the curved ones. "Architects sometimes want people to look at the building more than the art," she says.

Nuria takes me through the empty white spaces full of circular columns and cupped walls. It is as sterile as a hospital, as modern as a space ship. I ask her if she likes the building.

"It's good for the city. I like how modern it is."

"What about the neighborhood?" We walk outside to the new square next to the museum. "It doesn't really fit in."

"Look," she says and points at kids playing soccer and riding on skateboards and roller blades around the square. "They don't mind that it is here." Maybe it will fit in, this white space ship. Like the Pompidou Center in Paris which, after early resistance, has become almost as much a part of the old Les Halles district as the market itself was. Maybe opposites can coexist, the old and the new, the warmly familiar and the startlingly fresh.

Back in the Gothic quarter, I look at tiles in an antique shop on the Plaça del Pi. The shopkeeper tells me they are from the eighteenth century. They are heavy in my

Sailors, The Ramblas

hand, the colors mellow with age, the floral patterns soft and unmodern. People flood up and down the Ramblas. It is one of the world's great public spaces. It is ancient, but you can't find a better place to observe the world of today.

Two young women pass my café, wearing short skirts and high platform boots. Their teased hair is green and purple, their noses and lips studded with rings and jewels. No longer the newest look, it still has power. The women are fun to look at. They bring zip to the street, fizz to life. They are new china on an old table.

My mother breathes with the aid of a respirator. Her pneumonia has subsided. The liquid in her lungs has diminished. My brother tells me that she doesn't recognize him. Should I go home?

STREETS

The honeyed garden, the wild laughter, the braying horn. Only on foot can one get to know a city. The wrinkled face of the street sweeper, the bright eyes of the girl on a bicycle, evening light on crumbling wall. Walking urban streets is the best way to take in "the heady bouquet of the wine of life," to borrow a phrase from Baudelaire.

Lost in the otherworldly streets of the Gothic quarter, I listen for a moment to a plein-air Segovia. In an antique shop is a small eighteenth-century engraving of a plan for a town in the Pyrénées. It was so simple back then: build a square and put the church on one side, the town hall on the other with the market nearby and houses gathered around.

IS THIS OUR LOT?

The Ramblas follows what used to be one of the old Roman walls that enclosed the city, the wall itself having been built on the bed of a river. Rambla means riverbed in Arabic. It became a footpath in the eighteenth century. I walk down the Ramblas, the path of time itself, to the Boqueria market.

Saturday morning, the market is as busy as an ant colony. Baskets are filled with voluptuous fruits and vegetables. Graceful iron work crisscrosses overhead. People banter, bargain. Walking through the Boqueria market is serious pleasure. I buy some peaches and plums, watch a woman in a frilly frock filet a big fish.

In the afternoon, I see a mixed media installation of James Joyce's Dublin: the city as seen through the prism of the writer's life and fiction. I walk through a dark almost tunnel-like recreation of his house — the kitchen, his bedroom, his library. There is a pub and rooms of books and floors covered with old maps. It all has a hallucinatory, nightmarish quality. It culminates in a room filled with a globe of Dublin scenes reflected in mirrors changing and multiplying endlessly. The viewer is reflected too in this phantasmagoric revolving ball of images.

Are we all, like Joyce, turning topsy turvy in this world? Is this our lot: to be forever afloat in a stream of consciousness unable to make sense of anything? To grasp at all the world whirling around you, don't you first have to be standing still?

In a tiny restaurant behind the market, a young couple at the table next to me pulls out a packet of vacation photographs. As they eat, they pass back and forth pictures of themselves on a Mediterranean beach.

I am a voyeur, an outsider peering over shoulders. I am a traveler, in the world but not of it.

Boqueria Market

THE SPANISH PAINTER

Hernandez Pijuan lives with his wife and one or two of his four children in a flat on Carrer de Corsega just next to the Avinguda Diagonal in the Eixample. The flat is in a four-story Art Nouveau building with a wood and glass elevator. Hernandez is a painter. He has invited me for drinks.

"I was in Minneapolis once in summer and once in winter," he says, pouring Glenfiddich into a glass. "It was only ten below zero. The city has no character, eh?" He is tall with white curly hair set off nicely by his brown Spanish face and a dark green silk shirt. His thin expressive fingers play with tortoise shell glasses.

"Barcelona is more European, Madrid more Mexican. Barcelona is provincial. We spend a lot of time looking at our navel." To Hernandez, international art means American and German, provincial art means Spanish. "We have a few international artists," he says. "Tàpies, of course, Miró, Barceló."

It's warm in the living room. The noise of the city taps at the closed balcony windows. In the study at one end of the room, a wide modern desk stands in front of shelves and shelves of art books. "Franco did not censor painters such as Tàpies," Hernandez says. "He didn't understand their work and thought it harmless." He pours more Scotch. He has a deep raspy smoker's voice. The conversation goes into the night. He is forthright and warm but also disarming and shrewd.

Hernandez's wife arrives and sets sausage and cheese on a small round table, also gazpacho and a bottle of *rioja*. "I am sorry. It is a simple meal," she says. "Have as much of the soup as you like. We always have it in the refrigerator. It's fresh."

After dinner, Hernandez and I go to his studio on the top floor of the building. We look at his new paintings. "I have not seen them in three weeks," he says. They are on the floor stacked against the wall, painted sides hidden, the brown edges of the unpainted linen all that is showing. We look at each one and talk about it. They are abstract though inspired by landscape and nature. One has large black circles painted on a white ground.

"The circles refer to the round packets of hay in the fields," Hernandez says. Others have small black or brown circles or dots painted in wavering rows over the entire canvas except for two or three inches of border. The tactile surfaces are thick with paint, layers of white over black over green. "I always try to do something sensual, something spontaneous, something from nature. But it must have tension. I do not like intellectual, conceptual."

They are, I think, in their high abstraction rather conceptual. "There is something Arabic about them," I tell him. Well after midnight, we climb down the stairs from the studio. He gives me catalogs of his work. I take the clanky elevator down to the crowded streets and the warm summer night.

Tower, Old Town Hall

PRAGUE

WEDDING CAKE

I have heard that unspoiled, atmospheric Prague, arms open now to the West, has been discovered by the international young and that they have gathered here with their guitars, drugs, and backpacks, turning the city of Kafka into something vaguely like San Francisco in the sixties. Judging from what I see as I cross Charles Bridge, it is true. Clusters of people are gathered on the heavy cobblestones around a singer here, a violin player there. A group of kids gaze up at a dark-haired boy warbling a Cat Stevens song. Others lean against the rail beneath the black forbidding statues, smoking, drinking pilsner, and looking at the drab Vltava River. The mood is upbeat, communal, easy-going. It's a love-in.

Two men sit hunched in an old rowboat above the falls. They cast a line into the water from time to time. City lights glitter behind them. They have been sitting there for a thousand years. A gothic tower at the end of the bridge looms up before the Staré Mesto, the old town. It is as you imagined, Prague. It intrigues, seduces. Crowds move past the shops on Karlova Street into Old Town Square. The square is huge and crowded with buildings in colors and architectural styles that make your head spin. It is rich as wedding cake.

The facades are pink, green, and yellow, a mix and match of baroque pediments, neoclassical windows, Gothic porches. It's almost too much. Tyn Church, the clock tower, the Jan Hus sculpture, the House of the Stone Sheep, the House of the Golden Unicorn, the cobblestones, the floppy-eared horses, the buggies, the people. The buzz of discovery is in the air. We are all in on a secret

Darkness has fallen. The Czech names are confusing. I get lost on my way back to the bridge, lost as one is supposed to be in the gloomy maze of medieval streets. (To find your way, first get lost, the saying goes.) Eventually I find the river. The castle on the other side is lit up and so breathtaking in the pale green light, it seems staged. I gaze at it, entranced, like Gatsby before the light on Daisy's dock. On the bridge two men juggle batons of fire. Someone is playing a flute. A singer leads a group in a singalong. Everywhere the hat is out, everywhere the feeling of carnival. People are applauding. It is the Ramblas all over again, only in postcommunist Bohemia.

Charles Bridge

Orchestra, Old Town Square

CITY OF MUSIC

Concerts are touted endlessly in Prague. Shy hawkers hand out flyers, bright posters beckon from sooty walls. This is a city of music. The music halls are busy every night. And outside, along with cobblestone folksingers, are alfresco opera singers, forty-piece jazz orchestras on the square, oompah bands, string trios playing Dvorák in the arcades. Even groups of tourists go about singing with campfire voices.

On my way one evening into the Estates Theater, I stop to admire the fresh pistachio green walls of the newly renovated building. The premiere of Mozart's *Don Giovanni* took place here in 1787. I find a seat in the small chamber room off the main hall called the Mozart Cabinet. The program is predictable: Mozart, Smetana, and Dvorák. Who else would you want to hear on your first visit to Prague?

The room is elegant, hot, and sold out. The music, arias sung by a soprano and baritone from the Czech National Opera, aims to please, and it does. The pianist, a phlegmatic, kind-looking older man, is the object of the soprano's passion during one piece. She bestows a kiss on his red forehead as he plays. At intermission we are served champagne from trays and invited to see the fabled concert hall. We stand anxiously in boxes on the second and third floors and gaze into the hallowed darkness, barely able to make out the teal blue walls, the gigantic chandeliers, and the putti everywhere. "Saving electricity, I guess," one man says. With perfect timing, the lights come on to a loud collective "ahhh."

After dinner on Kampa Island, I walk the dusky, resonant streets of Malá Strana and think about the concert hall and the music. I call Texas. My mother seems to be better. She is going off the respirator. I call Minneapolis. There is a drought in the Midwest. "Cattle are dying, Dad," David says. The bridge is empty and quiet. The carnival is over for the day. The moon, orange and hazy and almost full, shines down on the dark sculptures.

MALA STRANA

From the taller of the two towers at the end of Charles Bridge, I look down on the city of Prague, at the Vltava coursing wisely between the Old Town on the east bank and the "lesser town" of Malá Strana and Prague Castle on the west. Charles Bridge connects, as it has for six hundred years, the two chambers of the city's heart.

Stepping off nondescript Malá Strana Square and into St. Nicholas Church, I am stunned, like a deer in the road, by the powerful beam of ornamentation — the gold leaf, the pink and green frescoes, the sensuous limbs of sculpted saints and painted cherubs. Today is Saturday, the exuberantly baroque church is empty, but two hundred years ago, had you sat in a pew, you could have heard Mozart play the organ. Or wept at the requiem sung here by a friend upon his death in Vienna. Across the square from the church is the huge Liechtenstein Palace. The Academy of Music, training ground for classical musicians, is located here. Loud rock and roll booms out as I pass by.

Pablo Neruda lifted his nom de plume from a nineteenth-century Czech writer, Jan Neruda, whose work he was fond of. Jan Neruda also gave his name to a picturesque Prague street. Nerudova Street goes uphill from Malá Strana Square toward the Hradcany district and the castle. It could be called "The Street of Houses with Lyrical Names." Up the thousand-year-old street are narrow baroque dwellings with names like "The House of the Three Violins," "The House of the Golden Chalice," "The House of the White Beetroot," and "The House of the Green Lobster." Jan Neruda's house is called "The House of the Two Suns." In the past a house was identified not by a number but by a sign, often illustrating the occupant's line of work. Other streets in old Prague have houses with charming names and signs, but Nerudova Street, with so many, is like a lane in a medieval fairy tale.

Rain slows the traveler. So does dark Czech beer. When the rain stops and the glass empties, I continue drifting through Malá Strana. Quiet, intimate squares are shaded by large trees, old palaces have been turned into embassies. Tricolored flags, not signs of violins, hang beneath balconies. Across from the French Embassy is the Lennon

Peace Wall. The singer's bearded face peers out beneath bright graffiti. Strange to find this in Prague, in such hushed surroundings — a shrine to a musician, a member of a band I was weaned on thirty years ago. Two or three young people sit near the wall, killing time. A guitar rests on the curb. Many people show up here on the anniversary of Lennon's death. Do the diplomats mind having this gaudy shrine in their genteel neighborhood? If only diplomacy crossed borders and knocked down cultural barriers as swiftly as popular music.

ALCHEMY

Prague Castle is a world unto itself. The castle and its buildings and grounds are vast, grown in the course of a thousand years from wooden fort and stone chapel to its current palatial size. Everything is here, from an imposing cathedral to the crown jewels to the bed of the president. Václav Havel slept here, as did Empress Maria Theresa, and Good King Wenceslas, who was sainted and buried in one of the cathedral's beautiful chapels.

Three seventeenth-century gentlemen were thrown out of one of the castle windows into the moat and survived because they landed in a pile of manure. The tossed happened to be Catholics, the tossers Protestants, and out of the incident (and the manure) the Thirty Years War sprang. Defenestration, the act of tossing somebody out a window, has always been a popular form of self-expression in Prague.

At the far reaches of the castle grounds is a narrow, ghetto-like street with tiny houses painted in bright colors. This is Zlatá ulicka, or Golden Lane. Now souvenir shops, the tiny houses (some have ceilings only four feet high) were in the eighteenth century the workshops of Prague's famous alchemists. If they failed in their attempts to make gold from lead, man from clay, the alchemists did achieve immortality. They, and their fellow scholars, magicians and cabalists, live on in legend if not in flesh because their dreams are our dreams, their fantasies our fantasies. One who kept the legend alive was Gustav Meyrinck. Meyrinck was a nineteenth-century German writer who wrote *The Golem*, a novel based on the Prague myth about a man-made monster. *The Golem* in turn became the basis of our century's most famous man-made monster, Frankenstein.

"When Gregor Samsa awoke one morning from troubled dreams he found himself transformed in his bed into a monstrous insect." The opening sentence of Kafka's story *Metamorphosis* is not about a monster made by a man but a man made into a monster. Is it Kafka's modernist take on *The Golem*? There are few lines more chilling in fiction. It seems appropriate that Kafka once lived on Golden Lane. His impossibly small house is painted a surprisingly cheerful blue. His work has roots in that irrational, I-can-make-the-impossible-happen world of eighteenth-century Prague. Kafka was, as are all great artists, an alchemist.

The artist's medium is "the golden light of metaphor," as Patricia Hampl puts it in *A Romantic Education*, her eloquent memoir about Prague. "The golden light of metaphor, which is the intelligence of poetry, was implicit in alchemical study. To change, magically, one substance into another, more valuable one is the ancient function of metaphor, as it was of alchemy."

In the castle is an exhibition of works by Czech photographers called "The Bitter Years." Black and white photographs from World War II cover the walls of a former palace turned gallery. They have titles like "Entry of German Troops Into Prague," "German Women Shorn of Their Hair," and "The Paving of Streets by German Women." To see pictures like this in Prague, in a city that really suffered in the war, is riveting.

Could the cause of World War II be attributed in some way to the suppression of alchemy in Prague hundreds of years ago? Hampl thinks so. She writes in her memoir that the attack on alchemy, which was as much about spiritual as material transformation, led to the devastating mind-spirit, science-religion split in Western consciousness. Rather than a united mind in which science and technology are connected to "the spiritual hunger that is their source," the Western world has seen the rise of rational thought which in its extreme form has "justified every atrocity in our immediate history: against Jews, against blacks, Asians, against the victims of the abstruse ideologies of Communism and anti-Communism." For Hampl the attack on alchemy was an attack on the imagination, on the fundamental need for metaphor. Then as now, she says, we live with a "fear of mystery, of the wisps of life that refuse to be pinned down, that will not make sense, that are irregular and do not fit."

THE WORLD'S MOST BEAUTIFUL AMUSEMENT PARK

At the Divadlo Comedie off Wenceslas Square are two one-act plays, *Protest* by Havel and *Permit* by Pavel Kohut, or is it the other way around? They are performed in English by a group of American and English actors. Staged with energy if not always skill, they are about life in the communist era. Havel's work is more interesting. It concerns the relationship between two writers, one a dissident who has been in prison, the other, a member of the establishment, who goes along with the system to keep his job and support his family. Though the established writer agonizes over his failure to protest and resents the dissident's smug moral superiority, he realizes he is more effective politically working behind the scenes even if it is less cathartic and dramatic.

In Old Town Square, lights shine in the turrets of Tyn Church. Like tides, people ebb and flow through the square and the maze of streets. A woman stands in a doorway, a crowd spellbound before her. She is singing *Ave Maria*. The castle glows on the hill like a holy place. Charles Bridge vibrates with the crowds, with sweeps of sound and pools of light. The river is gentle but mysterious. Children laugh, singers sing, old men and women eat ice cream.

From square to bridge to square to café to castle to church, by pale walls, bright windows, through the ancient gray streets of this city of music and carnival, we wander. Prague this summer night at the end of the twentieth century is the world's most beautiful amusement park.

THE FIRST TO DIE

On the stark white walls of the Pinkas Synagogue written by hand are the names of almost 80,000 Czech Jews who died in concentration camps. A woman behind a plastic cloth is rewriting names that came off during renovation. She writes the last name in red and the first name in black. She writes the date of birth and the date the person was sent to a camp. She is completely focused on her work. Watching her gives me the chills.

Outside the synagogue I follow a path around the wooded courtyard that is the old Jewish cemetery. It is tiny and hilly and packed with the dead. Over the centuries, as space gave out, soil was added and people were buried on top of each other, hence the mounds. Thousands of tombstones crowd and lean against each other in a casual but affecting way. Beneath these thousands are thousands more.

In the ceremonial hall of the Klaus Synagogue, across the cemetery from the Pinkas Synagogue, there is a small collection of drawings by children who lived and died in the Terezin concentration camp. The drawings are beautiful and full of life, miraculously unmindful of the horror around them. Terezin was not strictly a concentration camp but a transit camp for Jews being sent to Auschwitz. To the world the Nazis proclaimed it to be a model ghetto for "prominent" Jews, where life was lived normally complete with library, concerts, and cheerful paintings. Children were among the first to die because they represented the Jewish future (this I read in the book *In Memory's Kitchen*).

I walk down posh Parízská Trída (Paris Avenue) to Old Town Square where an English brass band plays to a large enthusiastic crowd. In another corner of the square, gymnasts jump and spin. How quickly scenes change, how strange to move from the silent confines of the cemetery to the expansive, garrulous square. A young girl asks for money. She's from Poland and can't exchange money, she says.

Jewish Cemetery

DINNER WITH VLADIMIR

A large crowd lounges at the foot of the huge and somewhat sinister-looking Jan Hus monument. The coal-like patina of this Rodinesque sculpture is a perfect reminder that Hus, radical theologian and Czech national hero, was burned at the stake. It is six o'clock. People gather to watch the tiny skeleton on the town hall clock toll the death knell as it does every hour. Prague walls are painted lovely pastels and the sound of music reverberates, but the dust of a morbid religiosity, centuries old, floats in the air. There are also a lot of bugs.

Under the town hall clock, I meet Vladimir. Not far from the square is the neighborhood of his childhood. He shows me his old home and school and a beautiful church. We go to a dark-tabled pub and have dinner: pork, dumplings, and sauerkraut. We drink dark beer. Vladimir is a jolly man in his late forties who works in the steel business. He lived in India for six years.

I ask him if the atmosphere in the pubs was different before the revolution.

"Not that different," he says. "People liked to eat and drink then just as they do now. And we have always liked to talk about politics."

He tells me about his life as a student in the early seventies. "I had a friend who was working with the KGB and I didn't know it. I think he told them things about me, that I had traveled to the U.S. and other things. I don't know what. The KGB interrogated me, tried to get me to become an informer. I refused, but I thought I might be forced to quit school. When the list of Czech informers was published after the revolution, I saw the name of my friend. I met him in the street one day and told him to go to hell."

I mention the Havel play I saw a couple of nights ago. "It was like that," Vladimir says. "You were always afraid someone would say something about you. You would lose your job or your chance to go to school. Many people were coerced to join the party. 'You have been chosen to be a member,' they would say. 'It's a privilege.'" He takes a sip of his beer. "You know about all this," he says, somewhat wearily.

"I've read about it. It's different when you hear it from someone who's lived it."

"Everything was censored," he continues. "We had world news at seven o'clock. From Moscow, Prague, Kraców, Warsaw. That was the world."

Vladimir eats with zest. He pulls his chair close and looks me in the eye. He radiates warmth and intelligence. "Most Czechs have a cottage in the country. During the communist years, we went to our cottages a lot. You couldn't trust anybody. You didn't know who was an informant and who wasn't. In the country you felt safer. We couldn't go to church. My son was baptized secretly. Now I want to make it official."

"What do you think of Havel?"

"I like him. He is the only one who could be president. He is still very popular though there is a lot of corruption. The black market is out of control. He has done some dumb things. He released prisoners. He should quit selling arms."

"How do you feel about the future?"

"We're going too fast. This is a crucial time. Everybody wants to be rich. To make up for the last forty years. Everything is becoming Americanized. You can get anything you want in the Czech Republic if you have money. There are lots of rich people. There is more crime. The gypsies work in groups pickpocketing on Wenceslas Square. Taxi drivers are thieves.

"Old people were hurt most by the change. They have small pensions, and the cost of living is going up. Children will benefit in the long run even though the cost of university is going up. I'm confident Czechs will become part of the modern world, the global economy. Before World War II, we were the thirteenth strongest nation. Some people think Czechoslovakia's golden time was the three hundred years of the Austro-Hungarian empire. Some think communism is better than democracy. I like it better this way."

"What about your future?"

"I want to move out to a village and live a quieter life. The city is too noisy and dirty for me now. When I was young I thought Prague was everything." He sets down his empty beer glass. "I'm getting too fat. Everything goes here." He points to his stomach.

BRIDGE

I linger for awhile on the bridge, watching the river, listening to a man playing a flute. It's after midnight. City lights still burn. Words and laughter from somewhere below the bridge rise on the soft breeze. A motor boat with a red light putters under the bridge. People on the bridge mill around in small groups. They are trying to decide whether

to call it a night or to dance on. My anonymity, my invisibility, is almost broken by two Czech boys. Bottles in hand, they lurch toward me, singing loudly. They stop and look at me. They look at each other, then shrug and break into more song. They are more amusing than obnoxious, more innocent than threatening. They are enjoying their visibility, their proud claim of the street.

It is while I am on Charles Bridge, near as I can tell, that my mother dies.

Night, Charles Bridge

Ferry in the Archipelago

SAME OLD WAY

"There is the lock," Pers Gothefors says, "that divides the fresh water from the salt water." We are atop a tower enjoying a panoramic view of watery Stockholm in high summer. Pers, a friend of a friend, is showing me the city. Islands spread as far as the eye can see. Boats are everywhere, some headed east toward the archipelago and Finland, others headed west toward Drottningholm Castle.

After the tour, on the balcony of Pers's pleasant apartment in the suburb of Nacka, we drink beer and nibble sausages. "I am going to be pensioned in the fall," he tells me. "I used to work with a union for Swedish academics. Now I work with the state. I am on the other side, with the employers."

We talk about cities. "Americans love old buildings," Pers says, smiling. He says that in the sixties and seventies Stockholm tore down old buildings around the historic center. "The new buildings were very bad and everybody was upset about it. Even here we do not always preserve the past." He tells me that once on a business trip to the Twin Cities, the driver of his car told him to roll up his window when they passed through a bad neighborhood. "Why do Americans not talk about the problems in their cities?"

"We talk about them. We just don't do anything about them."

"I never hear about the other side of America." Pers has gray hair combed forward, a red face and a protruding belly. His speaks English fluently, taking great care to use the precise word. "I keep searching in my mind and in my dictionary." He pushes his glasses back on his nose. The conversation turns to the square and human exchange.

"Television and radio are not real squares," he says, "because they operate only one way."

"The computer, the Internet goes two ways," I say.

"The computer will one day be like the telephone, an accepted part of everyday life. Now it's new, but soon everyone will be used to it and go on living their lives in the same old way."

I tell Pers about Sven Birkerts's book, *The Gutenberg Elegies*. "Birkerts thinks the computer will kill off the book, the traditional book. I worry that it will do the same to the city."

"It's such a nice summer night, isn't it?"

"Yes, it is."

"It's too nice to be pessimistic."

SUMMER PLACE

Beneath blue sky and bright sun, the crowded commuter ferry churns through the archipelago. It makes many stops. Mine is the island of Vinlo. Eye-catching boats are everywhere on the sparkling water: sailboats, tugboats, yachts, varnished wooden runabouts with blue and yellow flags. At each stop is a small dock with one or two people waiting, a welcoming grandfather, a mother and child. Large country homes and gardens are half-hidden in the green woods along the shore.

Waiting for me at the dock is Pers. We drive down narrow lanes through wildflowers to his little house. Chickadees, nuthatches, and other small birds flit about. I nearly step on a dead snake getting out of the car. "A city is not the buildings, it's the people," Pers told me when he extended the invitation. "If you want to understand Stockholm, you must go to the archipelago because that's where the people are, at least in summer. They go to their *sommarstalle*, their summer place. You must come to mine. It's on Vinlo. Wind Island."

Now driving through the woods he rhapsodizes about *sommarstalle*. "I love to listen to the sound of the wind, the rain, the birds. The sound of no sound – the stillness. This makes it possible to live in the city." Deep into the white night we talk. We sit outside with a bottle of aquavit and a plate of herring. The sky is as pale and clear as the aquavit even at midnight. As the sun wanes, Pers waxes eloquently on a range of topics. His red face glows in the dimming light.

On the welfare state: "Sweden used to be a prosperous country. Social Democrats are in trouble because they are telling us we have to cut our benefits. When someone is out of work here, he still gets his salary for a long time. Same with health coverage. There is no incentive to work. There is lots of abuse and fraud. Communists are gaining in power because they promise to keep benefits at the same level."

On communism: "The ideas behind communism are not dead."

On race: "What is race? It is just pigment. It is just the color of the skin. Africans are black because it protects their skin against the sun."

On crime and violence: "We have a lot of refugees from Bosnia and Lebanon, places where there is war. We can't take care of them as we should."

STORTORGET

Lennart Mork is Sweden's best known set designer. He works regularly at the Royal Opera and recently worked with the Washington Opera at the Kennedy Center. Lennart and I have drinks at a café on the small and lovely Stortorget in Gamla Stan. Balding, a little portly, he is a warm, talkative man full of enthusiasms and confidences. He wears glasses and has a thick moustache. He sips from a glass of white wine and sings the praises of Harvey Lichtenstein and the Brooklyn Academy of Music. Lennart designed the set for Ingmar Bergman's *The Winter's Tale* which recently played at BAM.

Lennart tells me he was working with Derek Walcott in Stockholm when it was announced that Walcott won the Nobel Prize. "Derek invited me to the award ceremony. The Swedish Academy meets in the Stock Exchange to decide who gets the prize. It's just there on the other side of the square. The square, Stortorget, is where Sweden began. In the early sixteenth century the Danish king slaughtered the Swedish nobility here. There was a bloodbath. Blood ran down the cobblestones and into the streets leading off the square. There was a rebellion and Sweden became an independent country."

At the fountain in the square, a child fills his hands with water spilling from the mouth of a gargoyle. Another eats ice cream. The square is blissfully serene. We talk about the state of theaters in Europe. Lennart is worried about cuts in the arts budget for Sweden. With great flourish, Lennart draws maps in my notebook and makes a list of things for me to see in Stockholm. "You must go to the subway stations," he says. "To see the art, the decoration. They are all through the city. I did one of them, at the Tekniska Högskolan stop."

We are joined by the choreographer Donya Feuer, a tiny, intense woman with silver hair and aquiline features. An American, she has built a distinguished career in Stockholm where she has lived for over thirty years. "I came here from New York to teach for three months and I stayed."

"She does the choreography for Ingmar Bergman's plays. She plots every move,"

Lennart says, "from the bending of the little finger to the big gesture." She recently received an award for "changing the dance culture in Stockholm" and has made a film called *The Dancer*, which is making the festival rounds in Europe to high praise.

"Gamla Stan is chic now," she says. "It's become touristy and noisy. It was run down when I moved here. They were going to tear it down."

Donya arranges for me to get a ticket to see Edward Albee's *Three Tall Women* at the Royal Dramatic Theater. Unfortunately the play is being staged in the small plain annex behind the Royal Theater's lavishly gilded main building. The play is sold out and I sit on a folding chair in the back. Margaretha Krook ("Sweden's Maggie Smith") has great presence; she commands the entire stage from the chair or bed where she is most of the time. The only word I can make out is "Arizona," and, despite Ms. Krook, I leave after intermission.

Back in Gamla Stan, in a restaurant on Stortorget I eat reindeer and lingonberries. To master the art of eating alone, it helps to eat in decent restaurants. Good food dispels loneliness. I have the narrow medieval streets practically to myself. The streetlights throw soft light off the cobblestones. Church bells ring. Opera descends from a third floor apartment. In a gallery window are a traveler's watercolors of faraway places.

CITY OF WATER

More park than garden, the Kungsträdgården (King's Garden) sits between the harbor and modern downtown. It was in the King's Garden in the sixties that Stockholm citizens protested against the wholesale destruction of the city's old buildings and gardens. Today it is full of people. Not just fair Swedes but Africans, Turks, Indians crowd the wide promenades and small outdoor cafés. Two shirtless men play chess on a giant board with bishops and knights the size of children.

Real children, black and white like the chess pieces, climb and hang from a jungle gym. Readers read in the grass, men on benches booze and snooze and occasionally leer, dogs sniff. A statuesque woman talks on a cell phone. Her big black dog pulls at its leash. It reminds me of my own. I stop to pat it and am instantly homesick.

The ferry to Drottningholm pulls away from the dock at city hall just as I run up. I poke around the city hall until the next ferry arrives. Built in the early twentieth century, it is made of red brick and has a tall imposing tower. It is, as I was told, "very solid, very Swedish," although when I think of something Swedish, I think of lightness not solidity, of blond furniture, pale blue eyes, and eighteenth-century Gustavian rooms. Inside is the great room where the Nobel Prize banquet is held.

The ferry moves slowly across Lake Mälaren, the "sweet" lake separated from the Baltic by the lock at Slussen. The engine rumbles. The afternoon sun is warm. We pass attractive new apartment buildings, many designed to look old, and banks of trees broken here and there by beaches of sand and rock filled with swimmers and sunbathers. There is something magical about passing through a city on a boat. Stockholm is very much a city of water.

"Look, there is the castle," a girl shouts.

A Drink of Water, Kungsträdgården

THE OPERA SINGER

The opera house at Drottningholm is closed. On a whim I ask a young woman at the museum if there is any way to get inside. I tell her that I am an artist and work in the theater and that I know Eskil Hemberg, the director of the Royal Opera. "Just a moment," the woman says. There is an exchange of phone calls. "Elisabeth Söderström will be here in a few minutes to give you a tour. She is the artistic director."

Before I know it the famous former opera star is shaking my hand. "Please excuse my appearance," she says. "I have just come from babysitting my grandchild." She is wearing a black T-shirt with the words "The Met" on it. Her eyes glow with warmth, her lips purse. She is an enthralling woman, refined but not stuffy, full of European graciousness and charm. "I have a little time to show you the opera house," she says. We cross a courtyard and she opens the door to an eighteenth-century world.

"The theater was built by Queen Louisa Ulrika who came from Prussia. She found Swedish culture appallingly bad. She brought French and Italian singers. It was designed by Carl Fredrik Adelcrantz. He was never paid. He was given quarters on the royal grounds, in the theater, I think. It is now a UNESCO cultural site."

Ms. Söderström points to a piece of dangling wallpaper. "That has bothered me since I started two years ago. I agreed to be directress for five years." The wallpaper with its delicate floral design is original. "There are two schools of thought. One wants to leave the theater as it is. The other wants to fix it up. The former is winning." She shows me a place on the door of the women's loo worn down by centuries of hands.

We climb stairs into the theater. "Go and sit in the middle," she tells me. Left alone for a few minutes to take in this extraordinary place, I sit on one of the benches in the house, which holds about four hundred people. The stage is lit at the moment and musicians are milling about. A fake door was added to one side of the stage to retain the perfect symmetry. The famous candles are lit. They used to be real candles. Modern ones were invented expressly for Drottningholm. They are electric but flicker in such a way as to look real. They "burn" during each performance.

"The audience is very close," the directress says as we walk on stage. "There is no line between fantasy and reality." The thirty-eight sets, most of them original, are painted flats that move in and out of the wings in the old-fashioned way. Drottningholm is the only theater in the world from the eighteenth century where the original set machinery is still in use and still operated by hand. "Directors don't want to work here. Each one I ask says the same thing: 'Do I have to use your sets?' They are wonderful but limiting." We go to the basement to see the wooden drums and hand-pulled ropes that lower the drops and move the flats.

Backstage the theater seems like a busy country house rambling but cozy. We chat with a singer in what feels more like a bedroom than a dressing room. In the courtyard I clasp the opera singer's hand and thank her.

"I must get back to my sandwich," she says.

"All my opera friends are going to be jealous."

"Tell them I am still on my feet." She laughs. "Would you like to be our guest at the opera tonight?"

The opera is *Tom Jones*. A quiet but persistent bell summons us from the gravel courtyard and the paneled lobby. I sit on one of the hard blue benches. The candles flicker above the orchestra's humorous wigs. A soprano in a vivid red and black dress sings silly words beautifully.

The scenery changes with each act from an interior to a garden to a pub. I have an odd vision of Elisabeth Söderström in her black "Met" T-shirt pulling hard on a rope below the stage. At intermission, the crowd, wine glasses in hand, shuffles out into the limpid night. Pebbles crunch underfoot. I mill around the pond, which "used to be a swamp." When the curtain falls, we stomp our feet on the wood floor. This way of showing approval is, like the candles, an old tradition at Drottningholm. It makes of us all children again.

THE END OF RESTLESSNESS

To walk is to contemplate, become philosophical, take the long view. Rousseau said that his mind worked only in conjunction with his legs, that he could think only when he walked. Walking is also escape. It is a way of avoiding, of turning your back. I sometimes think about what it would be like to do nothing but walk, to circle the globe on foot.

I take a long walk through the woods along the harbor. At Waldemarsudde, the house of Prince Eugen, there is a gallery of paintings by the prince and others, some of which are worth a look. Also charming, at least to me, are the old tile stoves all through the house. It is a hot day. Passing the many beautiful homes whose lawns roll down to the water, I am tempted to lie down in the shady yards.

I remember reading a book about a man who did nothing but walk. It was a kind of children's fable written by a German named Patrick Suskind. It was called *Mr. Summer's Story*. Mr. Summer walked day and night through his village and around the countryside because he suffered, it was thought, from claustrophobia, because he couldn't sit in his room. Once when he was offered a ride in pouring rain, he shouted, "Why can't you just leave me in peace?" Everyone thought he was crazy. Eventually Mr. Summer walked into a lake and never came out. Mr. Summer was an extreme version of Pascal's restless man. Or maybe he just carried restlessness to its logical conclusion.

Back toward town is Gröna Lund, Stockholm's venerable amusement park. Towheaded children squeal from inside whirling teacups and astride hand-painted horses. Teenagers eat cotton candy and wait in line for rides, which seem more imaginative and less terrifying than those in our carnivals. It is a remarkably clean and unsleazy place. I miss the deep-fried tawdriness of the American midway.

THE GOLDEN PEACE

Stockholm will be Europe's cultural capital in a few years. Annika Levin is organizing performing arts programs for the event. She is worried about funding because of the budget crisis. "Sweden has the greatest debt of Western countries," she tells me at lunch one day. A professional woman with lots of energy, she talks about living in Paris when she was young. "I moved there for love, what else? Restlessness is a function of age, isn't it? When you are young, you are restless. You grow out of it when you get older. I like having a house and a garden now. When I was young, I wanted to be in the city."

I walk through the tony part of town — by the opera, the Royal Theater, Sotheby's, the Grand Hotel, past the big tourist boats along the harbor. I have dinner in the oldest pub in Stockholm, a place where the painter Anders Zorn used to drink. The pub's name translates as "The Golden Peace." The Nobel Peace Prize committee comes here each year to wind down after picking the winner. It's a good place. My idea of peace tonight is a good meal.

I call Wendy. "Hello," she says. No matter how often I make a transatlantic call, I always think that it won't go through, that the miracle of instantly talking to someone thousands of miles away will not happen this time. She is just back from Chicago, tired and depressed after clearing out her father's house, which has sold. (He died last year.) David's wisdom teeth must come out. Sarah was at a party that got out of hand and the neighbors called the police.

Façade, East Berlin

BERLIN

THE PLACE TO BE

Christian Bauske steers his car through the streets of East Berlin. It is a pleasant evening in early August. The Reichstag, Brandenburg Gate, Checkpoint Charlie, Unter den Linden, Humboldt University, Potsdamer Platz. I am mesmerized by the sights and by Christian's high-speed, enthusiastic commentary. He talks nonstop in flawless English.

"I cried when the wall came down," he says. "We all remember where we were when we heard the news. November 11th, 1989." He talks about the difficulty and the excitement of trying to make the divided city whole again. "We have lost something that we will never regain. All the Jews are gone. We will never be able to recreate Berlin as it was before the war. But this is the place to be in Germany. This is an incredible time in history. I love Berlin."

We drive through dark streets of decaying buildings. We drive past new buildings and huge squares dotted with cranes. "East Berlin is rising from the dead," Christian says. "The cultural center was in East Berlin." Sooty, poor, strange and familiar as an old black and white photograph, East Berlin is much more appealing than modern, prosperous, staid West Berlin. At an outdoor café, we join people sitting at long tables drinking beer.

"I like the international flavor of Berlin," Christian says. "People speaking different languages." He is thirty-three, the managing editor of a weekly newspaper. "The paper used to be communist." He is a native of Frankfurt and studied law in Munich. "I got my doctorate at age thirty, but I didn't want to practice law so I went into publishing. I am thinking about getting an MBA in America."

He tells me rather proudly that he took part in this year's love parade. "I got into techno music," he says and laughs excitedly. "I never thought I would." Indeed, with his wire-rimmed glasses, polite manners, and intellectual air, you wouldn't think of him swooning over techno. He says that he liked Christo's wrapping of the Reichstag and that he spends a lot of time in Paris. "Germans have no *savoir vivre*." He laughs again. Christian is charming and smart, but it's his quick open laugh that makes him likable.

"I like to stay out late," he says as we pull up in front of my hotel at one-thirty. "Here is where we went tonight." He pulls out a pen and marks the places on a map. "You can go back and see them again at a more civilized pace." He laughs.

BERLIN WITHOUT THE WALL

At Brandenburg Gate, I buy a small photo collage with two tiny pieces of the wall attached to it. When I ask the vendor if they are really pieces of the wall, he says yes and shows me a photo of him chipping at the wall. As I walk away, he taps me on the shoulder and hands me the photo. "This was the wall. The pieces came from the wall. You take the photo. This was the real wall. Real."

The gate without the wall, of course, has lost its power. It is just another tourist site. Not many tourists are around this sunny morning. They browse through the T-shirts, postcards, and Russian army gear set up on tables as if at a rummage sale. They stop to watch a miming clown. They take pictures of the gate's horse-drawn chariot, but they also snap away at policemen on horseback. Standing between the Tiergarten and Unter den Linden, the neoclassical Brandenburg Gate has reclaimed its original life as the entrance to the broad avenue "under the limes" that once led to a castle. It is hard looking at the gate now to think of it as the sinister edifice of division it once was to Berliners. The goddess of victory atop the gate was mauled when the gate was swarmed in the celebration of 1989.

Pariser Platz used to be the square of foreign embassies. Now it is a blank except for the Adlon Hotel. A vast panorama set up in a covered rotunda shows what the barren plaza will look like in ten years. The large computer-generated designs depict a square of ultramodern high-tech office buildings that are chilling in their own right. They show images of smiling businessmen and pretty secretaries walking across the plaza surrounded on all sides by totalitarian façades of glass and steel. Is this another kind of wall?

WESTERN STYLE

Deep in East Berlin is the Kulturbraueri, an old brewery that has been converted into an art center. The rambling brick complex is about as far as you can get from the sleek future planned for Pariser Platz. I shake hands with Roger Pabst, a musician who is in charge of music programming at the center. I apologize for being late.

"Berlin is a big place," Roger says. "The *braueri* is hard to find." He is in his mid-thirties with sandy hair and bedroom eyes. He has a deep voice and the appealing scruffiness of an artist. He tells me, as he shows me around, that the Kulturbraueri is one of several art centers that sprang up in East Berlin after the wall fell. "Tacheles and Kulturhaus Bethanien are two others," he says. "They are more well known. We have plays, concerts, exhibitions."

"How is it going?"

"It's difficult to build an audience. We expected too much too fast after the fall. Government promised too much. Everybody was happy in the beginning. Now we are a little depressed."

We walk through ramshackle offices most of them empty. "It's summer. It's quiet around here." Roger pulls some brochures from a box. "Our budget is about five hundred thousand marks. Money from government is going down." We go to a café for a beer. "We are in Prenzlauer Berg. Lots of artists live in this area. It's poor. The rich live in the West, near the Ku'damm."

"What kind of music do you do?"

"I sing in the Frank Sinatra style." He mentions Joni Mitchell and Bruce Springsteen. "Popular bands try to sound like Bruce Springsteen." He tells me he is from a small town in East Germany about two hundred kilometers from Berlin. He is going there tonight for a family reunion.

"How do you feel about living in Germany now?"

"As a musician I like it. I like the freedom. But it is hard for us to get used to the Western style. It's more competitive, less sympathetic."

We wait together at a tram stop. He runs across the street to an ice cream shop and comes back with two cups of ice cream. He gives me one of the cups. He points out my stop on my map. He waits until I get on board. I wave and watch him walk away eating his ice cream.

A CITY WITH A RIVER

Berlin grew up on the banks of the Spree River in the thirteenth century. The Mitte quarter remains, despite the ravages of time and war, the historic heart of the city. The eighteenth-century opera house on Bebelplatz was wiped out twice in World War II. Across the platz is the old library with its concave front, like a "chest of drawers." On this square, in the early thirties, students enthrall to the new Nazi vision tossed thousands of books written by nonGermans into a bonfire.

A carnival is set up in the shadows of the Berlin Cathedral. Nearby is the baroque Zeughaus with its pink façade. The sun sets behind the Pergamon Museum and the Bode Museum on their island in the river. A city with a river is a wonderful thing. I think of the Mississippi, sadly neglected, running through the heart of Minneapolis. The storied Mississippi is just something we drive over.

The opulent buildings and the curving Spree give the Mitte an elegant if official air, but the desultory Soviet-era buildings along with a lack of street life conspire against the district's graciousness. Maybe new shops and the return of the grand old hotels will add some flair. It's almost dark when I arrive at the vast Alexanderplatz. The classical Fountain of Neptune and the Rotes Rathaus are in shadows. A neon Coca-Cola sign shines above the sea god's majestic head. A space age, star-scraping television tower looms above an ancient church steeple. Two rats scramble across the bricks in front of the town hall.

Spree River

Pool, Schloss Charlottenburg

SUNDAY IN THE PARK

Berlin is not a walking city. It's three times the size of Paris. If you like art, it is a city of feasts, though they are spread far and wide. In the Egyptian Museum is Nefertiti's head. Life size and one-eyed, it sits behind glass, serene and mysterious, an Arabic Mona Lisa.

The Schloss Charlottenburg has the greatest collection of Watteaus outside of France, including his wistful masterpiece, *Voyage of the Pilgrimmage to Cythera* (although there are two versions of this). Watteau's smaller *fêtes champêtres* I would take to the moon. Romantic paintings by artists like Carl Behlen and Caspar David Friedrich are in abundance. I have seen Friedrich's work only in reproduction. Though polar opposites of Watteau's amorous picnics, Friedrich's empty landscapes beckon me.

Speaking of picnics, blankets of food are visible throughout the castle grounds. The extensive gardens, playground to yesterday's nobles, have come in to public hands and on this hot Sunday afternoon the hands are many. Against the backdrop of the pastel palace, children romp in fountains, topless women sunbathe, matrons stroll geometric allées, men on bicycles coast over arched bridges. A network of formal hedges creates outdoor rooms. Appointed with benches, flowers, and sculpture, they have semi-private alcoves perfect for *les fêtes champêtres*.

Farther from the palace is the Belvedere, an extravagant teahouse with sugary green walls and gold cupola. The grounds are wilder, more natural. Boys kick soccer balls in an open field. A man snoozes, head in a woman's lap, on the edge of the tall grass. Seurat's *Sunday in the Park*, minus the monkey, has come to life.

I would love to come back one day and spread a blanket in the grass. As I head to the bus stop, a German woman asks me to take a picture of her and her daughter. "Allo," she calls out.

"I'm in a hurry."

"Please, can't you take our picture? One moment, please."

The little girl offers me candy when I hand back the camera.

The Wall, East Berlin

TOPOGRAPHY OF TERROR

Topography of Terror is the melodramatic name given to the vacant city block where the SS had its headquarters. The large lot of patchy grass in the midst of busy East Berlin remains empty as a way of remembering. On one corner of the block is an exhibition, whose facts and figures and photos recall the grisliness of the Nazi era but not as eloquently as the silent field.

Checkpoint Charlie is nothing but an empty lot, too, or next to one. Developers are at work here, and soon commerce will reign where once repression did. Nearby is a little museum of the wall. An exhibit called "From Gandhi to Walesca" overflows with paintings, artifacts, and videos about human rights and resistance movements. Where there is repression there is resistance.

The parts of the wall that are still standing are covered with graffiti and overgrown with weeds. To actually see the wall, or part of it, is a kind of catharsis. It has had since childhood a powerful grip on my generation's imagination. "The Wall" entered our collective consciousness in the sixties joining other goblins from the fifties: "The Bomb," "The War," "The Iron Curtain," "The Russians." We have been paranoid since grade school.

Potsdamer Platz in the heart of Berlin is a vast void. There is some life. Cranes span the plaza like a herd of giraffes. And Cirque de Soleil has pitched its big white tents on one edge. Black smoke billows up eerily through the necks of the cranes. I stop for a while at the memorial to Soviet soldiers who died in World War II then walk up the broad Strasse des 17 Juni and pass through Brandenburg Gate. To kill time, I walk along Unter den Linden before stopping outside the Russian Embassy. Here, like a character out of John le Carré, is where I am to meet Ilka.

ILKA

Ilka takes me in her little car to a restaurant in East Berlin called Brazil. She is a journalist for *Berliner Zeitung*, once the communist organ for the GDR, now owned by the large Hamburg publishing firm that owns *Stern*. "It has the largest circulation in Berlin," Ilka tells me. "Past readers still buy it out of habit. I write about social and cultural affairs. I am also interested in how the political affects the lives of ordinary people. I love my job."

Ilka has the self-assured air of a professional woman. In her early thirties, I would guess, she likes to talk and to listen. She studied history and politics in Munich and lived in Hamburg and in Paris for awhile. She was a fellow at the World Press Institute at Macalester College in St. Paul.

"I wouldn't live anywhere in Germany but Berlin," Ilka says, echoing what Christian Bauske told me earlier. "It is the only city that is interesting. Something important is taking place." She too cried when the wall came down. "Gorbachev was the one responsible for it."

East Germans are different, she tells me. "There is more of a community, more of a collective sense. It's not just rhetoric. They are not caught up in consumerism. It is hard for people now. There is no work, no money." She says it's difficult for East Germans to deal with the bureaucracy of the West. "In the East they knew how it worked. They were provided for in the major areas of their lives and lived off the black market for everything else. They understood their society. Now they have to learn new ways."

She says the East is much more interesting than the West. "The West is rich, bourgeois, and boring. It won't change. The East is being heavily developed and will probably become like the West. That's a pity. There's a ray of hope that it won't but only a ray.

"Art and theater are much more vibrant in the East. There is more possibility than quality though. The hot nightclubs change every week. They look for ruins. They are underground and strange and stay open all night."

Ilka says she wants to stay in Berlin. "It takes awhile to get to know the city, to feel at home. It is an aggressive place like New York. Berlin is unlike the rest of Germany in the same way New York is unlike the rest of the U.S." She says there is little racism and little crime in the city. "Foreign populations are well-integrated. We have the largest Turkish population outside of Turkey." The EC hasn't changed things much, she says. "Each country will keep its own language and traditions. Germans don't want to live in France and the French don't want to live in Germany. It will keep people from non-EC countries from coming into Europe, though, which is not good. The Vietnamese can't come in now. Western Europe will become sealed off and more prosperous." She asks me what I have noticed about Berlin.

"Cranes."

"What else?" she says, laughing.

"The feeling of energy. It's more at a boil than, say, Prague. Maybe because so much of Berlin was destroyed and it is in a sense starting over."

"What happens in Berlin in the next ten years will have an big effect on the future of cities," Ilka says. She looks at her watch. "Can I drop you at a taxi stand? It would take me an hour to take you to your hotel and drive back. Berlin is six times bigger than Paris."

"I thought it was three."

Berlin at night has a "racy, adventurous feel," as Fitzgerald once wrote about New York. It is bracing, emboldening, as many cities often are after dark. The taxi drives along Unter den Linden, by the illuminated buildings of the old center, through Brandenburg Gate, down the bright and busy Ku'damm. I am beginning to know the city, to make it mine.

A RELIGIOUS EXPERIENCE

At the Museum for European Art in the Kupferstichkabinett, or Drawings Cabinet, I ask to see some drawings. "You must sign in," a woman behind a counter says. Excited and nervous, I add my name and passport number to the list of professors and curators, those with legitimate scholarly business. I am ushered through a door into the inner sanctuary, into the study room. "What do you want to see?" a small man wearing white gloves and a lab technician's beige coat asks. The disdain is faint but distinct.

"Holbein, Cranach, Watteau," I say with authority. "Oh . . . and Botticelli's drawings for the *Inferno*."

I sit at a long modern table in a smallish room. Shades filter the light coming through the windows. A man at the other end of the table is studying a drawing, glasses propped on his shiny forehead, his nose sniffing the vellum. At another table two men in rumpled suits are whispering seditiously. The technician returns pushing a cart. On it are three boxes and a big book.

The clerk tells me how to look at the drawings. He opens a box and lifts a stack of fifteen or twenty matted drawings and places them on the left side, the cover side, of the box. He tells me to hold the drawing only at the sides and set it on the stand provided. "Look," he says. "You have only one hour. We are closing."

Botticelli's faint ink sketches of sins and sinners appear on the backside of Dante's Latin text. Three or four are in color, including the first page depicting the circles and Virgil and Dante descending. The Holbein portraits are the best. There are Cranach's "Lucretia" drawings and some religious scenes. The Watteaus are small, on brown or gray paper, done in brown ink, pencil, or chalk with body color.

Looking at these exquisite things is a religious experience. And a highly sensuous one. Your senses are heightened, concentrated. This is an act of great refinement, of great pleasure. The man brings another box, opens it on the table, takes out the drawings. I pick up one drawing centuries old, then another. I look and I look and the hour passes.

KAISER

At Kulturhaus Bethanien, an art center in Kreuzborg, is a young American woman with a spiky hairdo named Jennifer. She is from Chicago and is a visiting artist in residence at Bethanien. She invites me into her tiny messy room, both studio and living quarters, and offers me coffee. Large two-toned wingtips stick out from the bottom of her short pants. She introduces her boyfriend who is also from Chicago. His name is Turtle O'Toole. She also introduces a tall German boy. His name is Oliver Sartorius.

"I like Berlin," Jennifer says, "but I miss the multiracial flavor of Chicago." Oliver is from Heidelberg and is interested in film. He tells me he hates big-name German artists like Wenders, Fassbinder, and Kiefer, loves American junk food, and thinks German women have "too much weight and wear too little clothing."

The restaurant is a classic place, with the glow of old patina about it and a stylish, well-bred clientele. It serves good German food and is very well-known, I was told. The dashing owner seems to know everyone. The tablecloth is white. A candle burns in the cool night air.

It is the end of my trip. The owner calls me "Kaiser." A white Scottish terrier sits at my feet. A man plays classical guitar on the sidewalk. I look through my notebook. Like me, it is full. Words and pictures cover every page. On the first page are two lines:

"Go out into the world."

"To My Mother."

Jorg Ludwig calls to say goodbye while I am at breakfast. Jorg works at the American Embassy. He apologizes for not having had time to meet me. "One day it's art, the next day it's arms control. Berlin is the only place to be. History in the making."

Berlin Tegel is a cramped airport. No doubt it too will be overhauled in the history-making of the future. A bald, bearded security man runs his hands quickly up and down my weary legs.

"The brisk frisk."

"Pardon," he says. He draws his face up close to mine and says, "Have a good flight."

"Thank you. I will."

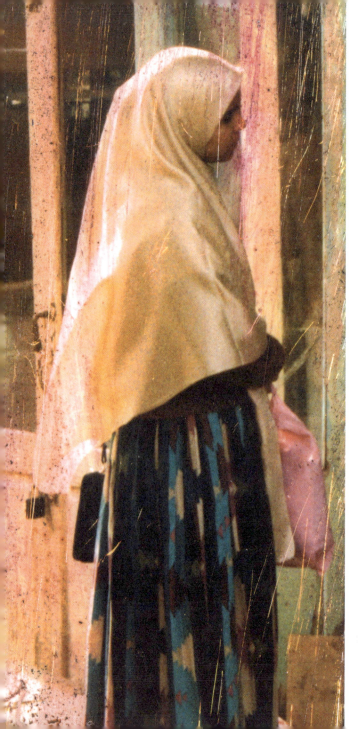

Young Woman, Cairo

COME AND GO

TOKYO	The Other Side of the World / Heart, Faintly Beating / Dogged That Does It / Fish / The Truest Things in Life / Gray City / Another Planet	171
KYOTO	Chopsticks / Temples / *Kaiseki* / Mr. Nakajima	182
DELHI	The Dark Scented Night / British Delhi / Connaught Place / The Future of Delhi / Fathers / Moonlight Square / Jama Masjid / I Belong to Delhi / Nothing Is Surprising	189
AGRA	Always / A Perverse Ballet	206
CAIRO	Eyes Open / *Sagesse* / The Egyptian Artist / *Shisha* / The British Critic / Soul / When All Is Said and Done / I Dream of Cairo / Pyramids / Flower Island / Come and Go	210
ISTANBUL	Land of Dreams / Ancient Places / Collective Delirium / I Hate Love / Alone But Not Lonely / Every Which Way / Grace / Eight Below / Taksim Square / A Night with Orhan / Russian Novel	233
MINNEAPOLIS	The Right Room	257

Street, Shinjuku

TOKYO

THE OTHER SIDE OF THE WORLD

The plane lands at Narita in a velvet fog. The sun has set. A day has been lost. Black-haired Japanese line up in rows at customs. On the bus ride into Tokyo, tall buildings, neon, water, glowing bridges, signs in Japanese appear randomly, slowly as if in a dream. A driver in uniform and white gloves ushers me into his spotless taxi. He drives on the left, English style. The door opens automatically when we reach my hotel. He writes on a clipboard with a pencil taken from a holder. The fare is 1,530 yen. I nearly pay 15,300. The hotel lobby is immense. I am whisked in my jet lag daze up a tall tower to a bland, Western-style room.

In the middle of the night, I hear the hushed creaking of the building. Japan is a place of earthquakes. I am on the twenty-second floor. I think of childhood homes to counter the strangeness of the room, of this long trip to the other side of the world. I look for something fixed to shake off the unreality of travel. The Pacific, unseen from the plane, was not real. Dark Tokyo outside my window does not seem real.

I think of bedrooms. The bedroom in the South Carolina farmhouse with the big bed where as a young boy I was allowed to sleep sinfully late. The veranda of our house in Greece where on hot nights my brothers and I dragged our blankets on to the cool tile to sleep beneath the stars. The paneled basement room my father built in Virginia, the bedroom of my teen years, and of the air-conditioned guest room in my mother's and father's house in muggy Corpus Christi. The sleeping porch in the Wisconsin cabin. How at night rain comes through the screens and at dawn a shockingly bright sun.

Memory is ballast. At times only the past seems real.

HEART, FAINTLY BEATING

Sitting near my table at breakfast is none other than the honorable mayor of Minneapolis. She is here on a trade mission. She and her entourage are not discussing trade but what to do with "Block E," the block in the center of downtown Minneapolis that has been empty for years. They are discussing, in other words, over scrambled eggs and French toast in a Tokyo hotel, how to revive the faintly beating heart of our city.

The Imperial Palace is hidden in a park surrounded by moats and gardens. A corner of it juts out from trees near one moat. Emperor Meiji built the palace in the nineteenth century where the castles of old shoguns once stood. The first castle was built on this site in the fifteenth century and marked the birth of the city. Castles came and went as did the original palace (destroyed by bombs in World War II and replaced in the sixties). The city changed its name from Edo to Tokyo, and its many millions are spread thickly around, but this spot remains the tenuous heart.

The palace is open only twice a year, but the grounds are a nice place to walk. I wander over bridges and down paths past pools of giant carp and groups of tiny elderly Japanese. A man in a formal gray coat escorts a woman in a kimono by immense blocks of stone that were once part of the old castle's foundation. Fan-shaped gingko leaves litter the ground. The November sky is blue, the wind cold.

Across the street from the palace is the National Museum of Modern Art. The museum is hot as a green house. Women guards in crisp uniforms sit attentively in chairs. Works by American and European artists are on display along with abstract works by Japanese artists in an exhibition optimistically titled *Singular Painting*. In the permanent collection galleries, paintings by Klee, Delaunay, and other Westerners hang side by side with paintings by their Japanese contemporaries. It is not always easy to distinguish Japanese modern from Western modern. The former looks a whole lot like the latter.

DOGGED THAT DOES IT

Shibuya is for the young and hip, but that doesn't stop me. The streets are crowded with shoppers and gangs of laughing school children. In the Tokyu Hands Department Store, I come across penmanship notebooks. The cover of one says in English: "Care and diligence bring luck. It is dogged that does it."

The Harajuku district's tree-lined streets are full of fancy shops and fashionable women pushing babies in strollers. I have a beer in the café of the Hanae Mori building designed by Kenzo Tange. I feel odd walking through the boutiques, but I want to see the elegant clothes of the designer, Hanae Mori.

Leaving the worldly pleasures of Harajuku for the quiet of the Meiji Jingu Shrine nearby, I pass through a gate of tall cypress trees into a vast park. Built in the early twentieth century to honor the Emperor Meiji, the shrine is made of cypress and has a sweeping copper roof. The shrine, like most everything in Tokyo, was bombed in the war and later rebuilt. Walking through this busy city, seeing it, feeling it firsthand, I think about the fact that fifty years ago it was rubble. It's amazing at how in such a short time Tokyo has risen from ash to cash, to become a place of (if not beauty) tremendous wealth, power, and energy.

Several women with yellow and white shopping bags are paying their respects at the shrine. Birds chirp sweetly in the thick woods, but a slew of screeching crows circling the shrine spoil the hallowed air. A young family arrives, daughter and son in kimonos. Grandparents are along to witness a rite of passage, the children's first formal visit to the shrine. There is a lot of picture taking, and much fuss is made over the sweet but puzzled children. As I stand there in the gathering dark, thinking how formidable the Japanese are, one of the crows spoils my hallowed hair.

FISH

The Tsukiji Fish Market — perhaps the world's largest — is located in a giant building on the Sumidagawa River. On a cold morning before dawn, I follow people and carts up a dock and through a door into another world. It is a crowded, hyperactive place. Men everywhere are stacking Styrofoam boxes of fish or pulling wagons loaded with boxes. Like oxen, they traipse through water-splashed aisles in black rubber boots. Others arrange displays of fish on ice. The brightly lit building is chilly and has the feeling of a convention hall or an indoor stadium. I give wide berth to the busy workers and am mostly ignored.

There must be a hundred different kinds of fish. Tuna, crab, octopus, squid, prawns, clams, scallops, snapper, mackerel, eel, shark, countless others, all pulled from the sea by Russians, Sri Lankans, Indonesians, Japanese. Most of it is flopping fresh, but a lot is frozen, including the tuna. Men in pink-stained aprons wield headless, tailless tuna around with hooks. They cut the frozen fish into hunks with chain saws. Most of the fish is auctioned off. A group of buyers standing on risers use rapid sign language to place bids. The auctioneer stands before them communicating in what sounds like grunts.

Bare light bulbs and colorful banners hang above the stalls. Restaurant people and shop owners fondle the fish on their beds of ice. The fishmongers have lined faces and red hands and wear toweled rings around their heads. They laugh and gesture with big sharp knives and toss weights to and from scales. Women in tiny cubicles smoke cigarettes and ring up sales.

An intriguing older man goes from one stall to another. He is wearing a blue bandana around his neck and is carrying a deep bamboo basket. He lifts a slender silver fish with a bright black eye, asks the fish seller a question. He doesn't have the brusque manner of the other buyers. Is he buying something for himself, I wonder, a sea bass or some scallops for dinner at home? Would that I could sit at his table tonight.

Tsukiji Fish Market

THE TRUEST THINGS IN LIFE

It's five in the morning. I am in bed reading *The Lady and the Monk*, Pico Iyer's book about love and Zen in Japan. "Zen," he writes, "was about slicing a clean sword through all the Gordian knots invented by the mind, plunging through all specious dualities — east and west, here and there, coming and going — to get to some core so urgent that its truth could not be doubted."

I would like to slice through the Gordian knot of here and there, home and the world, restlessness and stability. Iyer goes on: "None of the truest things in life — like love or faith — was arrived at by thinking; indeed, one could almost define the things that mattered as the ones that came as suddenly as thunder. Too often, the rational faculty tended only to rationalize, and intellect served only to put one in two minds, torn apart by second thoughts."

Pulling back the curtains, I am greeted by a brilliant blue sky and the golds and reds of the soft round trees encircling the Imperial Palace. Visible through the thick smog is a big Toyota sign. I hear the muffled rumbling of a train.

Outside the hotel, I see few children, few dogs, few signs of domestic life. This is central Tokyo, but few of the city's twelve million people live here. This area is made up mainly of the business district and the shops and restaurants of Ginza. Everyone knows about the five-dollar cup of coffee, but if you wanted to buy a few square meters of land in the heart of the city, in Ginza, say, it would cost over one million dollars.

I walk through Hibiya Park. It is a beautiful day, chrysanthemums and roses in glorious bloom, the air like a smooth sheet on the skin. The park is clean, seemingly safe. People are reading, sunning by the fountain, riding bicycles. A film crew begins to shoot a commercial or a scene in a movie by the fountain. A couple of down and out types lie on benches, sleeping off last night's excess. A dragonfly lands on one of them. The man snores as sunlight plays on gossamer wings.

GRAY CITY

Christopher Blasdel, an American, is director of the International House of Japan. He is also a musician, composer, and architecture buff. He takes me one afternoon on a tour of architecture in Tokyo. After a stop at the wonderful metropolitan gymnasium with its roof of silver metal shaped like an ancient warrior's helmet, we go to the smart-looking black and white striped Watari Museum of Contemporary Art, a small, privately owned museum designed by an Italian.

Other stops include the pre-war parliament building at one end of a boulevard of tapered gingko trees (much of Tokyo was like this — squat, stone, forbidding — before it was bombed) and a Noguchi garden in the lobby of a modern office building. The garden is masterful, but it looks a bit forlorn and out of place in the sterile lobby. Christopher was a friend of Noguchi's. "I met Isamu after one of my concerts."

We walk along woods surrounding the royal family's residence with Kenzo Tange's huge Otani Hotel looming in the distance. During a long taxi ride to Shinjuku, Christopher tells me he has lived in Japan for twenty years and is fluent in Japanese. "Sure the cost of living is high," he says, "but you can live well on less."

I mention *The Lady and the Monk*. "Iyer can't come for a year and think he knows a place," Christopher says. I sense that his resentment is directed not only at Iyer but at anyone who hasn't lived for a long time in a foreign country, as he has, and absorbed its culture. "The American community in Tokyo is an enclave, like a country club in the Midwest," he says.

The streets beneath the tall office buildings of Shinjuku teem with working Japanese. We head for the west side to the city hall complex designed by the ubiquitous Tange. At forty-eight stories it is one of Tokyo's tallest buildings and offices some thirteen thousand city workers. Some might say it is the center of the city now. Christopher calls the complex with its frilly windows supercilious. "Tange has lost touch with reality in his old age, like Kurosawa." It has a progammed, airless, space-age

feel. Indeed, the drabness, the futuristic quality of Tokyo itself is made abundantly clear as we look out through the haze at the gray city from the top of city hall.

We walk back toward Shinjuku through an underground arcade. Along one side is a row of cardboard boxes, a kind of shanty town of the homeless. Christopher takes me close to the boxes. Some are quite elaborately furnished with rugs and paintings and radios. Pairs of shoes are lined up neatly outside. A man greets us as we peer down into his box. This is the only sign I have seen of real poverty. "Many people think they should be forced to leave," Christopher says. "They are unclean." A rat scampers across the top of one box as he speaks.

We part at the subway. Christopher is soon swallowed up by the city he calls home. The sun is setting. I walk through Shinjuku, getting lost in the crowds and buildings brilliant with neon. I love the gauche signs, the high energy and crassness. It's not gray here, or quiet. Full of electronics stores, ramen shops, yakitori bars, strip joints, Shinjuku bursts with life. I go down one of the fifty or sixty entrances to the famous subway station and join the thousands of Japanese pushing their way on to a train.

Skyscraper, Shinjuku

ANOTHER PLANET

"I'm not like other Japanese. I'm from another planet. I like to party." This is the way Yuki Onishi describes herself to me on the phone. "Do you like to have fun?" she asks in a gravelly voice. I am a little taken aback, but we arrange to meet. When I arrive at the café in Roppongi, Yuki is sitting at a table with a young man. She has straight shoulder length lamp black hair, dark red lips and nails. We decide after talking for awhile over tea to have dinner in a sushi place nearby. Her friend's name is Akito; he is a university student.

Yuki went to college in Minnesota, was a roommate of a friend of mine. She is thirty years old and a dancer, though until recently she has been working at CNN. "I was a producer and director of news," she says, as we sit down on the floor of the restaurant. "Now I am working as a freelance interpreter and trip coordinator. I just took Stephen Hawkings around Kyoto."

A huge platter of raw fish is placed on the table before us. "Have you had abalone before?" Yuki asks. After dinner we go to a bar in Roppongi called Charleston, the first stop on what turns out to be an all-night affair. "*Gaijin* come here," Yuki says, nodding at the attractive, stylish foreigners sitting at many of the tables. "They are living or working in Tokyo."

We are joined by more of Yuki's coterie: two men, also university students, and two women closer to Yuki's age. They all speak English. There is much talk and laughter, much consumption of wine and cigarettes. Yuki is the ringleader and center of attention.

Next stop is a place called Bar, Isn't It? where we are frisked by big African-American bouncers. It's filled with Westerners and Australians drinking beer and dancing to loud music. We dance and drink, then flee to a quiet, atmospheric bar where there are paintings, Venetian lamps, and no *gaijin*. Yuki introduces me to the owner. We share plates of noodles, salad, and fish. The topic of conversation is exotic sexual practices of gays. Yuki clings to Hirogi, who has slicked hair and wants to be an actor. He is wearing a sleeveless T-shirt and a short wool scarf his mother knitted for him.

The other men, Tsuyoshi and Akito, talk to me about their studies, their uncertain plans for the future, the trials of living in Tokyo. Twenty years their elder, I must seem like an uncle to them. The women, perhaps because they have found places in the working world, are more confident and outgoing. Strong women, passive men, a contradiction of the traditional view of sexual politics in Japanese society.

On the street, I plead with Yuki. "It three a.m." She smiles and snaps a picture with her instamatic. "I'm Japanese. I take pictures." On a packed street in Roppongi, Yuki leads us into a bookstore. She takes a fashion magazine from the rack and sits on the floor beneath the fluorescent light. With her short black dress and black boots, she could have stepped from the pages of the magazine.

As we walk to her car, she talks about her recent breakup with her boyfriend. Yuki, the free spirit, is forlorn. "I believe in peace and love," she announces. "Guys get the wrong idea about me. I don't like sex. I like to make love." She snaps another picture. We drive through empty streets to another bar. It is very small with a trompe l'oeil painting on the wall and one or two people sitting at the bar. We sit at a table and order litchi nut drinks. Michael Jackson is playing. Yuki grabs Hirogi and begins to dance wildly. The rest of us watch and take pictures. "Isn't Michael Jackson a little passé?" I ask.

"We get everything fifteen years after the U.S.," Akito says. "We'll be conservative soon." The subway closes at one a.m., but instead of going home young people catch the first train at six or six-thirty in the morning. "We do this every weekend."

Hirogi wants to sit down, but Yuki keeps dancing, erotically running her hands up and down his body. Madonna is singing. When they sit down on the couch, she holds him in her arms. "Do you want to touch his breast?" she asks. Tsuyoshi, who would like to, cuddles with Yuki and Hirogi.

Dawn arrives along with a taxi. Yuki has to drive an hour to her parent's house where she is living. I worry about her driving. "Don't worry," she says. She kisses me goodbye. The rest of us pile into the taxi, which deposits me half an hour later at my hotel. Before climbing into bed, I call the front desk. The man laughs when I ask for a wake-up call at nine-thirty. "It's six-thirty," he says. "That's only three hours from now."

"I know," I say, "but I had a good time."

KYOTO

CHOPSTICKS

The blue nose of the bullet train eases into the Tokyo station. I am standing with others near a line on the platform marked with the number eight. When the train stops, the door of car eight is precisely at the line. The hum of the speeding *Shinkansen* is white noise, muffled, comforting, like a lot of Japanese life. The local train to Otsu, west of Kyoto, is not so quiet. I stand with my bags, a self-conscious giant *gaijin*, holding on to a pole. A young boy helps me find my way at the station and waves vigorously as I walk away. My kitschy high-rise hotel by a lake is full of Japanese leaf-peepers.

A player piano in the bar atop the hotel plays sappy Western songs over and over. A waitress kneels at my table and says that Beaujolais Nouveau has just arrived. A young woman takes over at the piano and plays stiffly as if in recital. She starts in on *Yesterday* as the wine arrives.

A paddleboat strung with lights appears suddenly on the black lake. The lights shine like stars in the dark water. It is a stunning image. Self-conscious again, I see myself, wandering American, sipping French wine in a Japanese hotel, listening to a Beatles tune, marveling at a scene that could have been concocted by Fellini. I am surprised by my reflection in the window. I laugh and lift my glass.

The sense of dislocation, of being a foreigner in a foreign land reappears at dinner. In one of the hotel's several restaurants, this one nicely decorated but empty on the thirty-sixth floor, I order tempura and sushi. The waitress hovers around the table, trying not to stare. I think I have committed some terrible traveler's faux pas. After a few minutes, she approaches me. She looks at my plate, at my hands.

"Good," she says in bold English. "You use chopsticks very good."

Calligrapher

Kyoto

TEMPLES

Ginkaku-ji Temple sits implacably in the rain at the base of the Higashiyama Mountains. Throngs climb the hill past the shops beneath waves of umbrellas. Now a Buddhist shrine, Ginkaku-ji was a shogun's villa in the fifteenth century and cultural center of the nation. It was famous for moon-viewing, flower-viewing, and incense parties. The garden, *Ginshaden*, is a two-foot high plateau of sand raked like sea in motion. The light of the moon when it rises over the mountain reflects off the sand. Next to this is a Mt. Fuji-like headless cone — the moon-viewing platform. Six feet high and sixteen feet in diameter, it is called *Kogetsudai*. I could take to moon-viewing pretty easily.

Another garden lies beyond. The rain deepens the fall reds and yellows and the melancholy of the place. Gardeners with weathered baskets and woven scoops work almost invisibly amid the moss, azaleas, and maples. I look for the "philosopher's path" where it is said a famous philosopher walked every day. It runs alongside a canal flanked with cherry trees and shrubs. Willow branches hover above the water. The muted colors are an ironic counterpoint. There is nothing muted about what I feel. The beauty, the feeling of being alone is overwhelming. I look at the houses along the street by the canal, thinking about Japanese families, about my own.

I visit the temple at the end of the path. It is tiny with a sculpture of a lion sitting in front of it and a place where one can write down a wish on a piece of paper. On the philosopher's path, I am happy to be alone. I have learned "how to populate my solitude," as Baudelaire wrote, but also "how to be alone in a busy crowd."

To Kiyomizu-dera, the grand dame of temples. Up long steps filled with shops and people. Children in uniforms are everywhere — boys in black suits, girls in short blue skirts and white bobby socks. The temple is one of the oldest in Kyoto (it dates from the eighth century), one that everybody visits. With its bell tower, giant pagoda painted traditional brilliant vermillion, and huge *hondo* made of cedar cantilevered on the side of a cliff overlooking Kyoto, no wonder it attracts big crowds.

The Japanese line up at the dragon fountain to drink purifying water from metal cups with long bamboo handles. And they line up at the "sound of feathers" waterfall which keeps illness away. The water falls in three streams into a pond. Beneath the streams, children, beloved Japanese children, stand next to friends and mothers and fathers and stick out long-handled cups. They laugh as the water splashes down into the cups and they laugh as they drink.

In the woods on the temple grounds, I can't find the Jinzo shrine dedicated to the *bodhisattva* who protects children, travelers, and the dead. My children, myself, my mother.

Kiyomizu-dera

KAISEKI

Sake is served in a gold ceramic shot glass. A kimono-clad woman puts the glass in my hand, takes the small flowered vase from a maroon lacquered plate and pours. I eat an appetizer of litchi nut, bean, and roe wrapped in a gingko leaf held together by a pine needle. This is *kaiseki*, an elaborate Japanese dinner served in *ryokans*.

Alone in my room, cross-legged on the matted floor, I am wearing a cotton *yukata* and tiny slippers that sit on my feet like dunce caps. On the enameled table in front of me is a vase of lilies. The *shoji* have been closed in front of the window to the garden. Paper lamps smile with soft light. The room has little furniture. It is elegant and serene, a place where time stops. I feel like a monk having his last meal, both holy and sybaritic.

The woman leaves her wooden shoes by the door and shuffles across the floor in her white socks and tight kimono. She brings dish after dish. Some are served together, others, brought out with even more ceremony, are served alone. Her lined, earthy face belies her ethereal manner. She smiles and bows and tells me the name of these delicious, mysterious foods. She speaks only Japanese.

I give up wanting to know exactly what I am eating and just enjoy the flavors and smells and the exquisiteness of the presentation. It is not knowledge but experience that I am after, to paraphrase Walter Benjamin. My notebook is a pale substitute for company. If only Wendy were sitting across from me. Here is a rough description of heaven on earth:

Miso soup with egg and crab.

Shrimp and pieced octopus served in a vinaigrette with delicately sliced cucumber and yellow snapdragons.

A broiled white fish, rather strong, served at room temperature on a piece of green bark.

Perched on a mint leaf, radish cut in the shape of a mum.

A soup of sausage dumpling wrapped in a thin blanket of egg and garnished with tiny carrot flowers.

Clams in a wine-dark bean sauce served inside what looks like a lime.

Another white fish, this one milder, accompanied by shitake mushrooms, scallions, and carrots.

Three kinds of olives all pierced by pine needles.

An orange-colored soup centered by a soft whitish root vegetable (parsnip or turnip perhaps) shaped like a top.

A big bowl of broth filled with sea bass and big hunks of white radish and the thinnest of lemon slices.

A pyramid of oysters bathed in a sweet milky sauce topped with radish shavings.

A condiment of sesame seed and small sprouts, another of chopped pickle, a third of a red fan-shaped vegetable.

Rice.

Tea smelling of hay poured from a blue and white pot.

As sweet, an orange fruit with dark seeds sliced like an apple and tasting of mango.

After dinner, the woman puts her hands like a ballerina to her cheek, and tilts her head. "Futon." Ceremoniously, she lays out the pad and duvet on the tatami. She puts the vase of lilies and a flashlight by the head of the bed. Bowing one last time, she disappears. Or vanishes, like a fairy into a gauzy otherworld. The only reminder of the real world, of tomorrow, is the Seiko alarm clock left by my bed.

MR. NAKAJIMA

I pass up a Japanese breakfast of fish and rice for orange juice, toast wrapped in paper, and my first coffee in a week. In the *Japan Times* ("Printed Without Fear or Favor"), there is an article about reducing the U.S. military presence in Okinawa. And news of a bomb, courtesy allegedly of Muslim militants, at the Egyptian Embassy in Pakistan killing fourteen, wounding sixteen. It is a gray morning.

The Nishiki Market runs through several blocks of central Kyoto. Its stalls are full of strange and wondrous things. In the hand of one vendor wearing a blue Minnesota Timberwolves sweatshirt is a turnip-like vegetable that looks like it might have been in my *kaiseki* dinner.

In the narrow streets of Gion, a truck gets stuck between two buildings, its tall sides caught as if in a vise between two walls. Cars and trucks are out of place in these old streets with their low-slung parched brown wooden buildings. Gion is a place for pedestrians and bicycles, an ancient place of slatted doors, cloth hanging in doorways, dark blinds covering windows, of secrecy, tradition, and beautiful shops.

In one tiny shop on Gion's Shinmonzen Street—the street of antiques—the owner, a delightful elfish man named Mr. Nakajima, offers me tea. He sits in stocking feet on the carpet, his short legs extended in front of him like a child. I sit one step down in a chair and listen rapt as an acolyte to his funny stories about life as an antique dealer. He mocks the pretense of the tea ceremony showing me all the while with great reverence ceramic tea cups specially wrapped in wooden boxes. He gives me a brief history of Japanese and Chinese art.

Mr. Nakajima relishes conversation. With his stuttering laugh, devilish eye, he certainly gives good company. He adds an "o" to words. He says "left-o" and "market-o." I tell him I will come back to Kyoto to see him.

"Come back before two years," he says. "Average Japanese live seventy-eight years. I born in 1919. I am seventy-six now. Not long to go-o." He laughs.

As he closes the door to his shop, I am seized by an urge to run my hand across the few white hairs that fly from his bald forehead.

DELHI

THE DARK SCENTED NIGHT

Security at Narita is tight. My bags are X-rayed twice, handchecked twice. I am frisked. Matchbooks are confiscated. ("Only one per passenger allowed on board.") I sign a disclaimer. The Air India jumbo jet is full, mostly of Japanese, some Indians, some Westerners. The first stop is Bangkok six-and-a-half hours away.

The flight attendants are dressed in saris and sandals. Brown midriffs, blood red nails. The nonsmoking section is every other row. When I cash traveler's checks in the Delhi airport, I am handed several packets of dirty rumpled bills. Each packet is two inches thick and contains one hundred fifty-rupee notes stapled together. There are thirty-four rupees to the dollar.

Mohan, the small unassuming driver for the American Institute of Indian Studies, greets me. We drive through the dark scented night from roundabout to roundabout. The streets are unexpectedly empty. The city is spacious, quiet, unlit. It is Delhi; it feels very foreign, and a little eerie. My hotel is fancy and crude at the same time. It is quiet on the seventeenth floor. What will it be like tomorrow on the streets below? In my notebook, I find a passage jotted down from V.S. Naipaul's *An Area of Darkness*.

"India is the poorest country in the world. Therefore, to see its poverty is to make an observation of no value; a thousand newcomers to the country before you have seen and said as you....Do not think that your anger and contempt are marks of your sensitivity....It is your surprise, your anger that denies them (the poor) their humanity."

I have come in a matter of hours from the land of haves to the land of have-nots.

Following pages: *Wall Painting, Delhi*

Boy with Monkeys, India Gate

BRITISH DELHI

The taxi driver is a withdrawn man with a beard and a green turban and watery red eyes. The taxi is a dilapidated black and yellow Morris, an Indian car from the fifties. The streets are full of them. We go to British Delhi, Luytens's Delhi: India Gate, the Rajpath, the presidential house, Connaught Circle. India Gate, a red sandstone monument to fallen soldiers, makes me think of Berlin's Brandenberg Gate. It stands alone (a gate to what?) in the middle of wide boulevards.

Schoolchildren, on a field trip, laugh and tease and cling to each other in the area around the gate. Vendors sell candy, toys, juice. One cooks corn. Two boys send their dancing monkeys out among the sparse crowd. A creaking blue bus passes, boys hanging out the window. A thin gray-haired man with a long white scarf tossed over his shoulder steers a tottering bicycle under the arch. I am the only Westerner. The monkeys dance for me, the lone stranger.

It's a mild November day. The sky is clear above the smog and dust. The vast Rajpath seems grandiloquent rather than grand, extravagant rather than generous. Was it colonial arrogance that put so much space in a poor crowded city at the service of pomp?

In the rear view mirror I see the driver's eyes close as we drive slowly up the Rajpath. Rhesus monkeys gambol on the lacy iron gate in front of the president's upright but whimsical house. It looks like an illustration in a child's book. In the garden are humorous topiaries — short green elephants and tall leafy birds. The gate is closed. There are no guards. I am the only one around.

CONNAUGHT PLACE

The heart of modern Delhi is Connaught Place, circular arcades of shops in near ruin. The Palika Bazaar is a seedy underground version of a Western mall. People approach to exchange money, sell postcards, shine shoes. One boy throws a glob of dung on my shoe. Before I know it my shoes are off and I am surrounded by a large group of kids. They clamor to shine my leather bag, stitch the strap of my camera case, sell me things. "Where are you from?" one asks. They are not entirely friendly. "Fifty dollars," the boy says when I ask how much the shoeshine is.

A small girl in rags begs for money as I walk to the taxi. "Please, please," she mumbles over and over. Finally, seated in the car, I give her some rupees. Immediately two or three other children materialize, their faces pressed against the window. Cars in the parking lot are jammed together like logs in an Oregon river. The driver pushes several away to make a path for his. Finally we are away.

A guard slips a mirror under the taxi as it enter the grounds of the Imperial Hotel. I have lunch at a table outside in a country club-like setting. The city rumbles beyond the garden walls. Birds are everywhere. Vultures in trees, green parrots with long tails. Pigeons wheel, sleek black and gray crows rake their beaks on the backs of the wicker chairs.

Thin men in olive uniforms tend the garden. Lissome women in brilliant green and brown saris, big bags balanced on their heads, cross the wide verdant lawn. Hotel guests and tourists eat and drink as shadows lengthen and the air cools. This could be a setting for a movie with heavy-handed almost laughable hints of the bad "isms" —tourism, colonialism, racism. As if on cue, the maitre d' slaps a mongrel dog that has ventured on to the terrace.

The Tibetan Market on Janpath is the hub of tourist Delhi. Stall after stall, tout after tout. On a side lane, less touristy, the yelling of the vendors is almost songlike. Harsh lights shine in the night. There is the buzz and bustle of barter and petty commerce. People swarm around a long table where a man has dumped bags of old clothes and fabric.

"Maps," a boy says, tugging at my sleeve. "Your price, your price." I pause at a bookstall with many books in English. I see copies of Forster's *A Passage to India*. From my hotel room I hear a band playing. A string of hazy lights hangs on the building where the music comes from. It sounds almost like reggae. I fall asleep to its strangely comforting pulse. The phone rings. A voice speaks in rapid English. "This is Gopi. I am a little unwell. Can we meet in a couple of days?"

THE FUTURE OF DELHI

I have breakfast with Dr. Mehendiratta at the Lodi Hotel. He picks me up in a chauffeured car. Dr. Mehendiratta is the gracious director of the American Institute of Indian Studies. He is small, balding, and wears glasses. His cell phone rings several times while we eat. He fusses with it but can't get it to work.

"What should I have?" I ask.

"I suggest *idli sambar*, *uttapam*, and maybe *masala dosa*. To give you a good sampling. This is south Indian food. It is more vegetarian." He eats with relish, or I should say chutney. Mint, red chili, and coconut.

Dr. Mehendiratta tells me he moved to Delhi from Pakistan after the partition of 1947. He has a wife and two grown children who live in Delhi. He launches into a rambling primer on religion and politics in India. "Sikhs wear turbans and have beards. Muslims have beards, but Hindus have no facial hair. This is usually the only way to tell the difference. You cannot tell in conversation, unless you ask. Hindus live and work together with Sikhs. There is not much intermarriage.

"The Muslims are not happy with the government. There was a bomb recently in Connaught Place. Muslim men can have five wives. They have many children. They prefer boys because girls require dowries. This is why we have overpopulation.

"India is attacked from three sides. Pakistan and Kashmir in the west. Bangladesh in the east and Sri Lanka in the south. Would you like some *sugi halwa*? It is a kind of sweet."

"Are you hopeful about the future of Delhi, of India?"

"Education is the way to solve our problems. We won't solve them in my lifetime, but in the next generation and beyond. People from rural areas are crowding into the cities. The population in Delhi was one million when I moved here almost fifty years ago. Now it's ten million. Too many people. We have too many people."

FATHERS

"I am twenty-two," Vinod tells me on the way to Humayun's tomb. Vinod is a thin handsome man from western India. He is my driver for the day. "I have five younger sisters." He asks how old I am. "You are strong. Can I have a cigarette? U.S. number one." I ask him to walk with me to the tomb. "I come once with my father," he says.

Humayun's tomb is on the list of things to see in Delhi because, along with the Red Fort, it is the best of the city's Mughal buildings. The first of the garden tombs (said to be the forerunner of the Taj Mahal), the massive seventeenth-century structure is made of red sandstone and has two domes, one inside the other. Arched walls decorated in white marble enclose the mausoleum. It sits on a platform in the middle of gardens divided into squares.

Humayun was an interesting man. The second Mughal ruler, he was more a student of science and lover of opium than he was a potentate. He died after a fall in his library. Vinod admires the marble dome and the Islamic grillwork in the windows. I love the burnt sienna of the sandstone.

"Humayun a strong man," Vinod says. "Father of Akbar. Akbar build the Taj Mahal."

"Wasn't it Shah...?" I start to say, but Vinod taps me on the shoulder and tells me to look back. The tomb is framed perfectly by the gate.

"My father show me."

"How long have you lived in Delhi?"

"Eleven years. Do you have children?"

"Yes." I offer him a cigarette.

"My father strong like you."

"Does he live in Delhi?"

"He is dead."

MOONLIGHT SQUARE

I spend the day rubbing up against a few of Delhi's millions. Dr. Mehendiratta introduces me to Amrit, a young poet who works in his office. "*Namaste*," she says to me, placing her hands together and nodding. Amrit is to be my escort. We go by car, inch by inch through gridlock traffic, to Chandni Chowk, the main artery leading into the heart of Old Delhi's bazaars.

Chandni Chowk was given its romantic name, "moonlight square," because moonlight reflected off the "stream of paradise" that flowed into it. A web of market streets and alley shops encircle it. Chandni Chowk is not for the claustrophobic. It completely belies its name. Once a royal boulevard, now the wide street is a dense, noisy, smelly welter of dark stalls, rickshaws, belching buses, sprawling dogs and cows, dirt, dust, and feces. Policemen with long sticks and machine guns patrol the area.

Amid the mass of humanity are schoolchildren wheeled along in wooden cages, coolies hauling big burlap bags on their backs, women in saris with nose rings and red *bindi*, Muslim women in *gurkas*, men in *kurta* pajamas and Ghandi hats. There are men pushing rickety bicycles, men getting shaved or getting their ears cleaned, men in bare feet passing time, talking, spitting, sleeping.

There is the jewelry market, the shoe market, the fish market. In the spice market, bags are topped up with coriander, turmeric, ginger, chili powder, peppercorns. Their tangy smells and tart colors seem the essence of India. There are prosperous shops selling rugs and wedding saris and clothes, and makeshift stands offering nuts, juices, popcorn, and *ghee*.

Amrit holds her arm in front of her, making a path for us. She tells me about the different foods and customs and bazaars. She shakes her head at the vendors who accost us at every step. She gives me a piece of *neem* bark to clean my teeth. She waits patiently while I take pictures. "I will write a poem about going to the market with an artist," she says. She has dark eyes and a sweet disposition.

"What does Amrit mean?" I ask. "Does it mean anything?"

"It means nectar," she says and smiles shyly.

Chandni Chowk

JAMA MASJID

Amrit and I go to Jama Masjid, India's biggest mosque. There is a circus nearby, and in a lot near the Red Fort, bus after bus pulls up packed with people from the countryside. On the other side of a wide crowded street, elephants stride through the throngs. The air smells of many things: smoldering rubber, incense, exhaust, spice, food cooking, garbage, leather, smoke, skin, dung. It's acrid, a little foul.

We walk up a steep hill to the mosque through a freewheeling open air market, clogged with people. It is Friday, prayer day. The city is extra crowded, Amrit says. The mosque of red sandstone and white marble dates from the mid-seventeenth century. Inside is a huge courtyard. We take off our shoes and hand them to a man behind a counter. People are scattered about, some praying, some mingling near the central pool, some chasing pigeons in the sunshine. It is a social place as much as a place for worship.

"The mosque was built by Shah Jahan," Amrit tells me. "It holds twenty thousand people. Mosques have no interior. Muslims come together to pray in the open."

My eye catches four young teenagers in brilliant saris, all different shades of red. They are in the main prayer hall under the domes on the west side (the Mecca side) of the courtyard. They seem tentative, laughing and whispering among themselves. They walk barefooted on the long rug, their saris flowing. After a while they stop in front of the shrine and fall prostrate, one next to the other, to pray.

In one corner of the mosque there is a shrine devoted to Muhammad. "His sandals are there," Amrit says, "and his footprint." As we leave the mosque, when I bend down to tie my shoe, I look twice at the bare foot of the man next to me. It has six toes.

I say goodbye to Amrit. "Thank you."

"It was my pleasure," she says. "*Namaste.*"

Later, walking in an arcade, I buy a pack of cigarettes from a man sitting at a table. His hand has two thumbs.

Jama Masjid

I BELONG TO DELHI

Gopi is in a state of pique. We are driving in his tiny car along the Rajpath. He is talking about how ugly Delhi is. "It was perhaps a beautiful city, but now it is beyond hope." Gopi Gaswani is a painter and graphic designer who works at the U.S.I.S. He is a small man, in his midfifties with longish graying hair. Expressive and kind (despite his venting at the moment), he suffers from migraines. We drive through the broad, shaded streets of the diplomatic enclave, past overbearing embassies on our way to the National Museum. "Politicians are corrupt. People have no discipline, no responsibility. They do not maintain anything, show no care for anything. Television and movies are full of sex and violence."

"Sounds like America."

"The U.S. is a great country. People who live in India in the country still have values. In the country life is pure and beautiful."

"Is it because of all the people, your troubles, Delhi's troubles?"

"No. People don't care, they aren't taught values. Families break down."

Gopi is Hindu but has many Muslim friends. He talks for awhile about India's history. "There is hostility among the different sects. Hostility is created by politicians, by extremists. It is imposed rather than innate. We can coexist peacefully if we are tolerant of other people's beliefs."

The museum is in bad shape. Works are badly hung and poorly lit. There are few titles. Gopi laments the shoddiness. We look at sculpture and ceramics from ancient India to the nineteenth century. Sculptures of Buddha and various gods and goddesses are primitive at first, more elaborate the more modern they become. Women, primitive or modern, are portrayed as voluptuous. The sculpture of southern India, usually of wood, is replete with fat nudes. "The eroticism in these works is healthy," Gopi says. "Unlike today when sex is sensationalized."

I am disappointed there are not more Mughal paintings, the delicate, precise miniatures depicting the worldly pleasures of old Muslim nobility. We have lunch at the India International Center. Gopi digs into Chinese food with his fingers. We talk about art in Delhi. "Galleries are like the museum. Not very professional, dirty, bad lighting. But there is a lot of art and theater here. Delhi is the cultural capital, Bombay the movie capital."

We stop for a moment at the Lodhi Tomb next to the center. Like the museum, the grounds are full of school children in uniforms. They walk in long trains, holding on to each other by the waist. Their dark-eyed, beautiful faces are full of life and laughter. People picnic in the grass. It is a day for picnicking, mild and sunny, a perfect winter's day in Delhi, not counting the smog.

Gopi drives back to my hotel through dimly lit streets of madding traffic. Lilac evening light, like fine spice, suffuses the city sky. "Lane driving is sane driving" pleads the sign on the back of the auto rickshaw in front of us. What lanes? "Can you get used to our ways?" Gopi asks.

"It might take some time. Would you ever leave the city?"

His eyes glaze over, he sighs a bittersweet sigh. "I belong to Delhi."

NOTHING IS SURPRISING

Sharon Lowen is an American expatriate and classical Indian dancer. She lives in a clunky building on Barakhamba Road. "Would you like to go to a fusion concert at the Taj Mahal Hotel?" she asks on the phone.

I climb the stairs to Sharon's small apartment. She is wearing a sari. She has dyed long black hair and sandalwood on her forehead. She introduces me to her teenage daughter who is drawing and watching an American television show. She takes me out on a huge veranda. "I have been living in India since the early seventies. I have made a name for myself as a dancer. I have a driver and a cook. I'm from Detroit."

Every square centimeter of the lobby in the Taj Mahal Hotel is covered in marble. "This is the fanciest five-star hotel in Delhi," Sharon says. The cocktail party before the concert is not gauche. It is full of elegant people: posh women making sari fashion statements, Englishmen in tailored suits, and young Indians in stylish *gurkas* and Western scarves. Drinks and lavish hors d'oeuvres are served on trays. "Hotels are a big part of social life," Sharon says. "Parties are always in hotels." The concert is a private, invitation-only affair. Sharon circulates easily.

The tabla player Zakar Hussain is the featured performer. He plays with a group of eight percussionists. "Zakar is famous," Sharon says. "He tours all over the world and is a big celebrity in India." We sit on cushions and pillows on the floor. There are maybe two hundred people in the room. The white-garbed musicians sit on the floor or on stools on a narrow stage.

The concert is superb. The players improvise in almost telepathic ways. They take turns, forming different arrangements of musicians and music. The young Hussain plays classical tabla, an older man plays *sarangi*. Some play southern instruments — a clay pot, a zither, a small tambourine-like drum. One man, who almost upstages the brilliant Hussain, plays a variety of drums and noisemakers with extraordinary virtuosity and spontaneity. Hussain speaks from time to time (in English). With his long black curly hair and boyish manner and large talent, he easily wins the crowd over.

Sharon nimbly wards off the advances of an English journalist as we leave the Taj Mahal. "Always friendly when they're sloshed."

"The best restaurants are in hotels," Sharon says as we go to dinner.

"That's surprising."

"Nothing is surprising in India."

Sharon tells me of her life in Delhi and of the struggle between staying and leaving. She runs the Indian studies program at the American school and wants to start her own performing arts center. She is divorced. Her mother comes every year for five or six months. She is a warm, easygoing woman.

"As a classical Indian dancer, I would have been peripheral in the U.S. Here not only am I in the mainstream, but I am considered one of the best dancers. I am accepted even though I am an American." She leans into her chicken tandoori. She ignores the silverware, in the manner of her adoptive land. "Besides I would have to be anorexic if I were a ballet dancer at home." She smiles and licks the *dahl* from her fingers.

"In the land of plenty you starve, in the land of hunger you eat," I say.

"Americans are obsessed with perfection, their strange idea of it."

We talk about the problem of settling, of home. "You have made a home for yourself in Minneapolis," she says in a maternal way.

As we leave the hotel, I comment on the contrast between the fancy crowd at the concert and the raw life on the streets. "Is there a real Delhi?"

"What's reality?" Sharon says lightheartedly. "Everything is an illusion. Reality, perfection, it's all illusion."

AGRA

ALWAYS

Nizamuddin Station is humming. It's seven in the morning. The sky is gray, the air cool. Waiting for the Taj Express near the tea stall, I am thinking about the head as conveyor. Muslim men walk along the platform with big aluminum trunks on their heads. I find my name on a computerized list stuck to the side of a car and take my reserved seat. The worn "luxury" train is full, with Indians mostly, some tourists for the three-hour trip to Agra.

The fields shimmer in the golden haze of early morning. Cows and goats graze, women lay fresh washed clothes on a riverbank. Skimpy trees are etched against the light. At the Agra station, I am assaulted by a horde of taxi drivers. They tug at my sleeve, yell and argue with each other. I settle on Arif, an older Muslim.

"You don't need a guide," Arif says as I leave the taxi for the Taj Mahal. "You can see everything with your own eyes. It is the seventh wonder of the world." The Taj Majal is a wonder that does not disappoint. On the long walk through the cypress trees I am drawn by the ghostly dome and minarets. My eyes go back and forth from the building's exquisite whiteness to its reflection, equally ethereal, in the channel of water before it.

Inside I join the line of people (shoes off) padding around the tomb of Shah Jahan's beloved wife. Her name was Mumtaz Mahal, "light of the palace." The emperor built the Taj Mahal for her after she died not yet forty in childbirth for the fourteenth time. The architect was an Indian named Ustad Ahmad, the chief mason was Iraqi, just two of the many thousands who worked on it.

The glass palace, as the mausoleum is called, is bathed in filtered light. All is hushed. Magnificent latticed marble screens surround the cenotaph, actually a false marble casket (the empress is buried twenty feet below). The tomb is a marvel of *pietra dura* inlay, precious stones in floral designs set in soft marble. The king, imprisoned in his

Women, Taj Mahal

dying days by his grasping sons at Agra Fort, could not set foot here. But every day, the legend goes, he would look out from a tower in the fort at his beloved's resting place across the Yamuna River. The Taj Mahal became his resting place, too. The two tombs sit side by side.

Outside under a brilliant blue sky I walk around the porches. The milk-white marble, fair as the fairest skin, seems the perfect material for a monument to love and memory. The florid Persian calligraphy adorning the walls along with the jeweled flowers and arabesques seem the very word and picture of adoration. It seems fitting that the place is full of women. They come, young and old, in flowing scarves and saris along the pool toward the whiteness. They cross patterned tile terraces, some hand in hand, and enter the hushed chamber of devotion. To be so loved, they say, to be so adored.

I can imagine my mother, my sentimental, romantic mother, coming here by herself, in a sari even, to see this heavenly temple and to lay a flower at the tomb of the mythic beloved. She signed her letters to my father, "Always." As he signed his to her.

A PERVERSE BALLET

Arif's taxi winds through streets of inestimable poverty and filth, scenes of primitive peasant life. Animals roam willy-nilly, bony holy cows, scruffy goats, pigs, and dogs. Bicycles, rickshaws, scooters, trucks, collapsing buses, camel and bullock carts, the occasional car, all weave nonstop in and out almost in slow motion. There's a strange choreography to it; it's a kind of perverse ballet. Horns sound, near misses take place by the second.

Unchanged for centuries, it seems, despite the presence of motorized traffic, the street life is rich and poor at once. Brilliant saris and turbans, naked children, painted carts, and wall advertisements flash amid the food stalls and barbers and mechanics. One woman carries a basket on her head filled with large briquettes of cow dung. We pass a brass band in a park, musicians in maroon uniforms blowing away. A man with a long black beard moves rapidly through traffic on his hands. He has no legs.

"I will stop so you can see the baby Taj," Arif says. I get out of the car and wait while a boy with a stick and a string of dark steers amble by. I clamber down a reeking riverbank and look out. The stench is overwhelming. To my right, not far off, a man is defecating in the mud.

Minutes come and go slowly on the digital clock at the station. A one-legged boy hops by like mad, the stub of his leg sticking out from khaki shorts. An old woman sits, a baby in her pile of skirts, and begs. I flash back to the young woman embracing her radiant child at the Taj Mahal. I remember the purity of the white marble.

The express back to Delhi comes to an inexplicable halt a few minutes out of Agra. We move on then stop again. This happens several times. The conductor hassles a Dutch backpacker about his ticket as the train stops for the fourth time.

"You are supposed to have a reservation," the conductor says.

"I have a reservation," the backpacker says.

"Not for the express."

The Dutchman looks out the window of the stopped train and around at the nearby passengers. "Is this an express?" he says and grins.

CAIRO

EYES OPEN

Mohan drives through quiet predawn streets to Indira Gandhi Airport. He asks me to replace a badly torn fifty-rupee note, which was among bills I gave him when I arrived. "Too much is missing," he says. Could the same be said of India?

The Gulf Air plane flies over the Persian Gulf, brown mountains, lifeless desert. An Arab man in a beard and long white robe sleeps across from me. His big brown foot sticks out into the aisle. "Your first time?" one of the flight attendants asks, spotting my guidebook. "Cairo is a nice place. I'm sure you are going to keep your eyes open." I am not reading about Cairo. I am thinking about Delhi, about India.

Red sandstone, turbans and beards, Gopi's soft voice, Zakar Hussain, the gaze of a princess in a Mughal miniature, the power of Islam, flies, two thumbs and six toes. Like a dream, India dances in the mind, first here, then there. Beauty then shoddiness, exquisite sari then glob of dung, shy "*Namaste*" then surly beggar, carved marble then reeking riverbank. India is a place that shines through dust, a place that defies easy comprehension.

We stop in Abu Dhabi and Doha before landing midafternoon in Cairo. "Keep your eyes open," the flight attendant says and flashes a dazzling smile.

"Mister David?" the tiny man asks. He has thick glasses and a heavy accent. "Give me your passport. I am Samir."

Samir is the public relations man for the museum sponsoring the art critics' conference in Cairo. He takes care of customs and carries my bag to a small bus that he drives to a hotel in Zamalek. He points out buildings along the way, newly built mosques, the President's home, big hotels along the Nile. "Cairo is modern," he says, proudly. "Men dress Western. Fifteen million people, three million cars."

Dervish, Zamalek

SAGESSE

The art critics' conference is held on Zamalek in a former mansion that is now the Great Cairo Library. I am greeted by a Cairene woman with big sunglasses and a husky voice. Her name is Fatma Ismail. She works for The Center for Art in Cairo and is one of the organizers of the conference. I remind her that I am an artist not a critic.

"All the better," she says, running her fingers through her short swept back hair. "We don't have anyone from the U.S." A scarf sits on her shoulder like a parrot. She puts her arm in mine and introduces me to other participants milling around a large hall: Jala, a critic from Ankara, a rather severe-looking artist from Syria, a curator from Rotterdam, as well as several members of the Egyptian art community.

We sit in a small room around tables with name cards and microphones. My name is in Arabic. The few audience members sit in folding chairs. The moderator is Dr. Moustafa El-Razzaz, a small, benevolent man. The topic is not benevolent: "Technology and Its Impact on Artist, Critic, and Recipient." Dr. Moustafa asks me to speak. "You have just traveled around the world," he says and smiles. "Tell us what you have seen and how new technology is affecting the art world in America."

I launch into a disjointed speech about the onslaught of the digital age. Everything I say is translated into Arabic. The other panelists join in. Change is inevitable, we all agree. Do we accept or fear the computer and the Internet? I want to dwell on what will be lost, on the notion that life as we know it is changing irrevocably. Others are more willing to embrace change. "We have to make it work the right way," Jala says. "We have to humanize it, to 'aestheticize' it." She is a feisty woman who speaks out against Western society imposing itself on other cultures.

One panelist, rebuffing me, says fear of technology, is romantic, nostalgic. Dr. Moustafa says it is bourgeois to want to handle old manuscripts. Artists of the future will be different, another panelist says. They will have to know how to manipulate pictures on a computer. They will be "photoprogrammers."

Thomas Mayer, the Dutchman, talks about how video is becoming more widespread and sophisticated. Jacques Leenhart, a French critic, says the world is image-oriented now, image-saturated. Critics and teachers will have to help people master the volume of images, to "read" them for their political and social and ideological content.

Microphones make people omniscient. There are many eye-glazing speeches. The air is thick with art theory. The poor translators work fast and furiously. During the welcome break, we mingle in the ornate lobby, cigarettes and Nescafé or tea in hand. I chat easily with the other panelists. Artists approach with catalogs.

A woman artist tells me Cairo is a hospitable place. It has been a crossroads for centuries. "We welcome strangers. We have *sagesse*, wisdom of the ages."

Khan el-Khalili

THE EGYPTIAN ARTIST

"You are nervous," Fatma says and laughs a throaty laugh, "because I am a woman."

"I am nervous because you drive like a man," Jacques says and flicks cigarette ash out the window of the tiny car. Cramped in the back seat, Thomas and I hold on for dear life as Fatma wheels cavalierly through Cairo's rush hour.

In an old quarter of the city we walk through a labyrinth of shops and dark alleys. In one doorway a girl nurses a lamb. Between alleys boys play ping-pong beneath a bare light bulb. We are going for an evening session of the conference to the studio of Muhammed Abla, a prominent Egyptian artist. The studio is in what was once a lavish home built in the eighteenth century. The carved wood ceilings are twenty feet high and in the center is a defunct fountain from which three large open rooms branch off. Abla, who shares the studio with three other artists, has placed his work around the rooms.

It is an extraordinary place, heavy with age and decay. Abla is a stout, confident man in his early forties, with thick curly hair and a bushy moustache. He is direct almost to the point of bluntness. He shows slides and talks about his life. He has lived and worked abroad, shown and sold his work in Europe. He is married to a Swiss woman.

Abla has had a more international career than other Egyptian artists and talks at length about not fitting in either in Egypt or Europe. He works in a number of styles, figurative, abstract, mixed. His work has Egyptian themes but it looks Western. His decision not to work in one style reflects his nomadic lifestyle, he says.

Several on the panel and in the audience criticize him for this shifting approach, for not being true to his native land. Indeed much of the evening's discussion revolves around the identity crisis of Egyptian artists: the struggle to find a way of dealing with the history and culture of their country and with that of the Western world. Jacques goes on at length about "the plight of the Third World artist in the First World." Jala argues for an "Eastern" style. "We do not have to be subject to Western traditions."

SHISHA

It's Thursday night. People are out in Khan el-Khalili, drinking tea in the cafés, smoking *shisha*, buying bread and vegetables, playing pool. Tomorrow is Friday, holy day. Thursday night in Cairo is like Friday or Saturday night in Chicago. Through festive streets buoyant with color and life, we walk. We feel festive too. The evening session is over. No more speeches. The night air is mild. Every now and then there is a blast of nasal music and voices grow louder.

We settle into a big circle next to a high brick wall outside a café, maybe twenty of us, just come from an artist's studio. Tea is served all around and in front of Abla a hookah pipe is placed. "Would you like some hummus?" says a bald man sitting next to me. "Your first time in Cairo?"

"Yes."

"Welcome. I am El-Nashar, the artist. This is Ali, one of my students."

"Welcome," Ali says. He looks like a noble in a Faiyum portrait. "I would like to visit America. Can I send you pictures of my work?"

"David," Fatma calls from across the circle. "Have some *shisha*." Abla hands me the tube. "Welcome," he says. Like a child, I suck and watch coals flare in the little pan and the water bubble. "After a while you forget all your troubles," Abla says. "Keep sucking."

The apple tobacco doesn't seem to have much effect, but the night air and the festive Cairo streets and the brown faces and this circle of welcome make me delirious. I am bubbling with contentment. "This is my wife," El-Nashar says. He is standing over me, motioning to the woman next to him. I look at them with the pipe still in my mouth. "We know a wonderful pizzeria on Zamalek. Would you like to join us?"

THE BRITISH CRITIC

Martin Gayford, a British critic, appears in the hotel lobby in dark suit and blue tennis shoes, carrying a copy of the *Rough Guide*. Martin is about forty, lanky, with dark bushy eyebrows. He lives in Cambridge and writes about art for the London papers and the British magazine, *Modern Painters*.

"An American once told me I was too polite to be a critic."

"Aren't the British born polite?"

Martin is appealingly awkward and speaks in a quick mumble. "Did that chap Samir meet you at the airport? I had no idea who he was, but I gave him my passport as ordered and he promptly disappeared. Two seconds later a man from American Express greeted me. He also asked for my passport. My knees went weak. 'Oh, my God,' I said. 'I've walked off the plane in Cairo and given my passport to a complete stranger.'" He thumbs through his guidebook. "My wife comes tomorrow. We are going down the Nile. I hope her plane makes it." He has a look of mock terror on his face. "Fear of flying. Me not her." The taxi swerves then stops. "I also have a fear of Cairene drivers. *Shukran.*" Martin hands the driver some piasters. "Let's get out of here."

He is more at ease in the museum. He reads to me from the guidebook as we walk through halls of primitive architectural fragments, textiles, icons, and manuscripts. "Copts, Egyptian Christians, date from the early centuries after Christ. It was the dominant religion before Islam. There are six to eight million now in Egypt." We linger over a Bible written in both Coptic and Arabic.

Claustrophobic Coptic churches are huddled together in the fortress-like quarter. Built and rebuilt over the centuries, they are age itself; they press in on you. Their interiors, though depleted by the neighboring museum, entice and haunt. I rub my hand over the immense carved doors, look long at the plaintive icons, the dark stained glass, the windows of carved lattice.

On the way back to Zamalek, Martin talks about the English art world. He tells me about how the odd and naughty Francis Bacon upended a table on Giacometti and once insulted Princess Margaret when she sang Cole Porter songs at a party.

SOUL

Midan at-Tahrir, or Liberation Square, is Cairo's main square. I pass a sign with the name written in Arabic and in English. In English, it says simply The Square. Is this what I have been looking for in city after city? The square of squares? Not quite. For starters, Liberation Square is not a square but a circle, or an approximation of a circle. And, apart from the Egyptian Museum, which anchors one side, it is a rather unpleasant place. Another anchor is Cairo's main government building, so big and ugly it is hard to contemplate. Egypt's impenetrable bureaucracy is second to none, it is said. One guidebook claims that a light shaft in the building acts as a waste basket and is filled several stories high with paper.

The square is busy with cars and buses and, yes, people, but people are definitely second fiddle to the storms of traffic. There is greenery amid all the concrete and bad architecture, but the place is so vast and assaulting and thick with exhaust, all you want to do is flee. Three boys with a soccer ball run up and say hello. They want me to take a picture. They are all smiles and athletic braggadocio. Cairo is such a soulful place, why is its center so utterly soulless?

Previous pages: *Cairo Traffic*

Sign, Liberation Square

WHEN ALL IS SAID AND DONE

El-Nashar invites me to his home on Zamalek to see his paintings. He greets me at the door as his wife brings out bread and cheese. The apartment is small but comfortable. "We have lived here for thirty years," El-Nashar says and pours Scotch into glasses. "We spend summers in Alexandria." We look for a few minutes at his wife's oversweet paintings then go to his cramped studio.

El-Nashar is in his midsixties, earthy and talkative. He laughs heartily, often rubbing his bald head. One eyebrow juts out an odd angle. Two pairs of glasses hang on chains from his neck. "There are three schools of art in Egypt," he says and takes off his glasses. "One is only Egyptian and is conservative. One is Egyptian and modern. The third is not Egyptian. I do not like Abla's work. Not Egyptian."

El-Nashar thinks his own work is clearly of the second school. He paints geometric designs or naturalistic motifs on canvases stretched over shaped blocks of wood that fit together like puzzles or mosaics. The roughly executed work has a strong three-dimensional quality. They are reminiscent of Islamic decorative textiles and screens.

"It is Eastern but in a new way, contemporary. My work has to reflect Egypt but also the universe. It must have mystery." El Nashar takes off one pair of glasses and puts on the other. He looks hard at the painting before us. "I hate acrylic. I paint only in oil. Don't you hate acrylic?" He reminds me of Hernandez, the painter in Barcelona. Like the Spanish painter, he is older, established, full of vitality. He is needy, worried about his work, self-involved, as are all who create. "I am having a show at the Center of Art," he says proudly. "Seventy pieces. A kind of retrospective."

He shows me some earlier figurative work. "These are about war. War with Israel. Very different from what I do now." He points to a large mosaic work in which he has combined elements of mirror, fabric, gold, and silver with painted designs and hieroglyphics.

"Are you getting more Egyptian in your...?" I ask, hesitating.

"In my old age," he says and laughs loudly. "Yes, perhaps I am. When all is said and done you go back to your roots."

He walks me back to my hotel. The night air is chilly, surprising after the warmth of El-Nashar's apartment, the Scotch, and the easy garrulousness of the man himself. "It was a very enjoyable evening," he says, shaking my hand and squeezing my arm. "You are always welcome in Cairo, in my home."

I DREAM OF CAIRO

We are on our way to see pyramids, Moustafa and I. Saqqara is the first stop. I am sitting in the front seat of Moustafa's car next to the driver, Ahmed, one of Moustafa's students. Moustafa, plump, jolly, loquacious, is holding forth from the back seat. A born teacher, he is giving me a lesson in Egyptian history.

Leaving the city behind, we follow a canal through barren but picturesque rural landscape. The leisured calm of the country, the tranquil timeless scenes of life on the edge of the desert are hypnotic. Peasants work small plots along the canal. A man in a gray *djellabah* leads a donkey carrying a load of bright green hay and a laughing young boy. Women in scarves wash clothes in the canal though much of it is covered with a thick invasive green weed. Camels peer at us from dirt fields, children look up from games in front of painted stucco houses. A sign on the road reads "Good life, happiness, and immortality are found in Egypt."

Ahmed parks the car outside the entrance to Saqqara, one of the necropolises (along with Giza) of Memphis. It seems the middle of nowhere. Sand is all around. Both a soldier and his camel look down with scorn. We walk through a door in a wall, pass through a long colonnade, and enter a big sandy courtyard. We are in the city of the dead: the funeral complex that grew up around the pharaoh Djoser, who founded the city of Memphis.

Djoser was buried in the first pyramid ever constructed. It is a series of six huge flat tombs, or "mastabas," lying like steps one on top of the other. Built some 4,500 years ago, it is one of the oldest buildings in the world and the first significant building to be made of stone. The hands of time have rounded the pyramid's putty-colored stones and the sides of each layer, or step. The ancient structure has all the charm and vulnerability of a many-tiered mud cake or yesterday's sand castle. It also has unspeakable dignity.

We enter a tomb and walk through narrow but well lit passageways. Moustafa points to the beautiful reliefs that run along a three-foot wide band on the walls. If much has been lost, much has survived miraculously, mostly as fragments. There are

scenes of people fishing, hunting, caring for animals. There are pictures of boats, tools, baskets. The graceful depiction of arms and legs, intertwined flowers and animals is unaffected and human.

The colors in some of the reliefs are strong — bold blacks and reds — but in most they are pale chalky tones. The powdery residue that clings to the walls is all the more powerful and eloquent for its softness. After thousands of years, after millions of days these muted, anonymous pictures in this clammy tomb settle on the eyes like breath and speak not of death but of life.

In the car, Moustafa's discourses on life in modern Egypt. "We are a nonviolent society. People talk to each other here, care about each other. If I went to the park alone to meditate, people would come up to me and ask me what's wrong." We bounce along the road past men with shovels and picks. Moustafa speaks again, softly, as if to himself. "When I am away from Cairo for a long time, I dream of Cairo."

Pyramids, Giza

PYRAMIDS

It is late afternoon when we arrive in Giza. We have driven hurriedly from Saqqara across a bumpy dusty road. Time is running short. "I'm sorry," Moustafa says. "We won't be able to stay long." Children, donkeys, and men on camels part to let the car pass. I walk around for a while a bit overwhelmed not only by the pyramids but by the carnival-like atmosphere and the city hovering at my back. These of course are **the** pyramids, the famous trio of tombs built for the pharaohs, Khufu, his son Khafre, and Menkaure. Keeping watch over the necropolis is the Sphinx, which like the Queen of England has to be seen to be believed.

The pyramids are especially powerful in relation to each other and to the rolling dunes of desert beyond. Against the desert backdrop all their mystery and eloquence and timelessness come to the fore. The perfect simplicity of their forms and their size (the Great Pyramid is eight hundred feet at bottom and five hundred feet tall) require scale, lots of it, and a bare bones setting. In the pink gray light of evening, riders on horseback race across the sand and Bedouins swaddled in long colorful scarves sit atop loping camels.

It's only when you spy the mobs of people clamoring in the foreground or turn around to see a modern suburb of Cairo creeping up that the scene turns a little sour. The red of the smallest pyramid strikes a tragic note somehow. The Sphinx in the dusty twilight appears feminine and sad, its terribly eroded face out of sorts with its virile, lion-like body. The face is supposed to be the face of King Khafre, but it seems to me the face of a stoic heartbroken woman.

FLOWER ISLAND

Muhammed Abla waits in front of the Egyptian Museum. We drive to his apartment in a working-class neighborhood ten minutes from the museum. Abla's wife, a teacher, and two children are at school. Remains of breakfast sit on a table in the large foyer. In the dark sitting room there is a television, cushions piled around the floor, and paintings and prints by Egyptian and European artists on the walls. Interesting objects are scattered about: an old Egyptian mask, a fragment of carved wood, a piece of black basalt with Arabic writing. The view from the second story window is of shuttered windows, clothes drying, streets crowded with people.

On the street, Abla stops at a fruit and vegetable stand to buy some bananas. Piled high are figs, dates, olives, nuts, artichokes, oranges, melons, grapes, mandarins, the bananas, plus apples from Washington. Egypt imports most of its food. Still it's surprising to see apples in this ancient quarter plucked from an orchard in Wenatchee.

After a tour of the Islamic Museum and Ibn Tulun mosque, Abla says mysteriously, "We go to see Cairo from another view." He waves at a passing taxi. Around us the city of Mahfouz swarms. Streets overflow with traffic, people, animals. A border of rotting garbage runs along one curving avenue. Men in *djellabahs* and *takias* (white lace skull caps) and women in *hijabs* (the scarf falls to the waist or is tossed over a shoulder) are everywhere. People carry trays piled high with pocket bread or pots of tea. Hole-in-the-wall shops are filled with bamboo boxes of live chickens and ducks, cartons upon cartons of eggs, fresh fruit hanging in nets. Brightly painted carts are loaded with vegetables. Camels stride down the street with the cars, donkeys munch nonchalantly. Horns honk endlessly, people cross the street at any spot in the constant, overwhelming traffic.

Finally a taxi stops. We creep across the city. I ask if this is normal for Cairo.

"Everything is normal in Cairo," Abla says. He gives the driver a banana.

Finally free of the taxi, we cross a busy street and board a small wooden boat filled with peasants carrying bags of food. A boy rows the boat slowly across a short span of water to an island. We walk on a dirt lane past a hut and a stall of donkeys to a

Bread, Cairo Market

green field about the size of a small city lot. There is a small reed hut at one end of it. It is surrounded by other green fields. This field, this lot belongs to Abla. "I am going to build a house here," he says.

All around the pulsing city looms, but here it is idyllic, quiet, arcadian. This island— it is called Flower Island — is a kind of paradise in the heart of the city. "Wherever I go, I always look for the country," Abla says. He pumps a well, digs paths in the dirt with his hands to allow water to reach a couple of scrawny young trees. "I am planting lemon trees." A girl from a nearby house brings a reed mat and pillow and a pot of tea. A man appears with a hoe and digs holes for more trees, to complete the orchard. In a field, a man cuts tall grass with a sickle. Children pile it on a donkey cart. It is a lovely day, sunny and mild. It does not seem like December. The stress and crowding and noise of the city fade away.

Abla has a quiet power. He needs both city and country. Though distant and somewhat taciturn, he has allowed me however briefly into his life. We cross back over the channel. He gives the boatboy a banana. We part in different taxis. The driver offers me a cigarette as we cross the Nile in the soft light of the setting sun. This time I succumb to the pleading of the shoeshine boy outside the hotel.

COME AND GO

Fatma is vivacious, a quality my mother liked in a woman. She is theatrical and a little skittish. Her smile reveals cloud white teeth. She is wearing a jean jacket and black boots. The conference is over. She is in a celebratory mood. We are sitting in El-Fishawi, the famous café in Khan el-Khalili. Tea is served steeped in mint. Fatma fills my cup then hers. "In Egypt the woman does everything for the man. Shall we order *shisha*?"

The café is crowded. Mixing at liberty among the patrons are shoeshine men, newspaper sellers, girls swinging incense, children hawking Kleenex, wallets, lighters. "It's open all night," Fatma says. "Mahfouz doesn't come here anymore, of course. He's too old." I look at the reflection of interesting faces and flurry of life in the mirror behind her. El-Fishawi's walls of mirrors confuse and expand the space. At one moment, casually glancing into a mirror across the room, I see a man with a tube in his mouth and a grin on his face who looks remarkably like me.

"I travel abroad a lot," she says. "I like to go, but I like to come back. Tell me more about yourself, David. Stop asking so many questions."

"Does this stuff actually do anything?" I look into the smoldering cup of tobacco and apple.

"They say it does. I just like the act of smoking it. I don't do it very often. Women usually don't do it at all."

"You have done well, Fatma, especially in a world where you have to pour tea."

"It is a man's world. I am very much a woman. A woman who likes her *shisha*."

Next to the big mosque outside the café is a colorful Egyptian tent. Bright bulbs hang over a wailing Muslim cleric and a crowd sitting in mourning. Later, standing on the balcony of my room looking in vain for the Nile in the dark, I think about what Fatma said. "I like to go, but I like to come back."

ISTANBUL

LAND OF DREAMS

The taxi follows the curve of the Bosphorus through the chilly, wet night. My hotel, a wooden confection Granny Smith green, sits in the shadow of Hagia Sophia and Topkapi Palace. An Englishman and his wife drink champagne in the lobby before a fire. The cold air of Byzantium rushes through the bedroom window. It smells of coal and spice and smoke. I can see the minarets of the Blue Mosque. I have entered the land of dreams.

The Blue Mosque, bathed in light, is visible from the window of the restaurant where I have dinner. The restaurant is named after a famous Turkish impressionist whose paintings adorn the walls. In an intimate room with a candle on the table, I eat eggplant and grape leaves and meat and pocket bread and drink raw Turkish wine and thick Turkish coffee. Every now and then the lights of the chandelier dim. A calico cat rubs against my leg, mews up at me. It needs a companion.

The wind is bitterly cold. Somehow it adds to the romance of the night, or the missed romance. The streets are empty, the carpet shops locked up. The domes and minarets of the Blue Mosque glow serenely, mysteriously in the inky sky.

An empty streetcar sits on a hill. Its lights are on, but there is no one in it, not even a driver. There is no one around. The wind picks up, the rain falls harder. A man passes, his face hidden by a wool cap and the upturned collar of his heavy coat. Suddenly I feel bare, frighteningly, emotionally bare, and alone. I feel far away from everything I know and love. I long for family, friends, the warmth of home, but for something else, too, something deeper.

The rain lets up. The Blue Mosque grows more ethereal, more beautiful. It is somehow consoling. I walk on.

Blue Mosque

ANCIENT PLACES

Dawn. A muezzin cries out, summoning the faithful, or maybe it's the less faithful, to prayer. His amplified nasal song shocks me from sleep. The winter garden behind the hotel emerges from darkness. In the lovely courtyard a rose-breasted dove sits in a large bare tree along with a chickadee. On the street horn blasts from boats on the Bosphorus carry through the cold, clear air. In one direction are minarets, in another gulls sweeping. Istanbul in the light of day.

The Blue Mosque looks glorious in the morning sun. Shoes off, I walk gingerly along the carpeted floor staring at the tiles, like a child in a zoo. There are thousands of them. This sea of Iznik tiles is what gives the mosque its name – they're all blue, a rich, dreamy blue. Lights hang from the dome by the dozens, a modern and seemingly unnecessary intrusion as the seventeenth-century mosque is filled with natural light that glides through stained glass windows.

Hagia Sophia is the dowdy ancestor of the Blue Mosque. Hagia Sophia means "divine wisdom." From the outside, it is a massive heavy-looking structure, from the inside, a soaring architectural wonder. The gigantic dome is extraordinary as are, to a lesser degree, the marble walls, Byzantine mosaics, and flowered column capitals. The building is dark, cold on this winter's day, and a little forbidding as truly ancient places often are. There is something reassuring about old buildings. They take me out of my own over-worried moment in time and carry me back.

Justinian, the Byzantine emperor and leader of Constantinople in its prime, built Hagia Sophia as a church in the sixth century. In the fifteenth century, under the Sultan Muhammad, the Ottoman Turk who conquered Constantinople and changed its name to Istanbul, minarets were added and it became a mosque. The Christian mosaics were discovered and redisplayed only in the twentieth century. That ceramic depictions of Christ and Mary coexist with wooden plaques inscribed in Arabic script with the names of Allah and other Islamic religious figures is another of history's nice twists. Of course, Christians and Muslims do not pray here side by side. Hagia Sophia is a museum now.

Iznik Tiles

COLLECTIVE DELIRIUM

The Pera Palace is the elegant turn of the century hotel that catered to passengers of the fabled Orient Express. Greta Garbo, Mata Hari, and Sarah Bernhardt stayed here. It is where Agatha Christie wrote *Murder on the Orient Express*. The Pera Palace is in the grand hotel tradition, but there is a sort of homey charm underneath the grandeur. I have a drink in the hotel's busy bar decorated with tiny artificial Christmas trees before meeting Don Terpstra, next door at the American Consulate.

Don, the public affairs officer, has invited me to a party at the home of the consulate. "You'll get to meet some interesting people," Don says. "Turkish and American." He is thin and pleasant and has badly bitten nails. "I've been in Turkey a little over a year," he says. "I'm originally from La Crosse, Wisconsin. I'm a Lutheran a long way from home."

We pick up a woman who works at the American embassy in Ankara. "I got out of Indiana as fast as I could," she says.

The house of the consulate is a fancy but rather sterile place overlooking the Bosphorus. A huge Asian scroll covers one wall in the living room, which fills quickly with embassy people, journalists, and assorted Istanbul illuminati. The consulate himself is a tall, bald man from Minnesota. Wine and trays of hors d'oeuvres circulate. An acrid cloud of cigarette smoke rises above the noisy crowd.

I meet several Turkish journalists. They are expressive men, hearty, forthright, who kiss each other on both cheeks. They talk with passion about Turkish politics and the issues of the day: "Islamic fundamentalism is on the rise." "Fundamentalists oppose joining the EC." "Kurds should have the same rights as Turks." "She is not very effective or popular and may not get reelected." "Inflation is high and investment has stopped since she became president." "The military is a big force in our government."

One of the men is Sammy Cohen, who writes for *Time* and is considered the grandfather of Turkish journalists. A tiny man with sparkling eyes, he is quite accustomed to regaling. "Istanbul is a city of villages," he tells me. "People come from the country, but they do not adopt city values. They retain the values and beliefs of their roots.

In fifty years Istanbul has grown from seven hundred thousand to twelve million."

Ara Guber, the photographer whose pictures of Istanbul are acclaimed throughout the country, is a crusty, bearded pasha who stares right through me. "Istanbul has become very ugly and modern," he says. Another man with thick glasses pokes his finger in my chest and blows smoke toward the ceiling. "Istanbul," he rhapsodizes. "I'll tell you what Istanbul is. It is a collective delirium."

At the end of the party, Don discovers that the consulate has disappeared. "I can't believe it. He took our driver." He is angry and embarrassed.

"He went to the Marine Club," a Turkish woman says. Dressed in a long coat and black hot pants, she slurs her words and leans against a wall. "I know another party we can go to."

The ride back to the city seems interminable though the car travels at breakneck speed. The driver stops to buy a bottle of Scotch and a bag of chips. "Ataturk's boat," he says, pointing to a big white yacht docked in the river. "Private now. You can rent. A thousand dollars a day."

I HATE LOVE

Serap Mahmati appears magically, in the Turkish way, on a street corner not far from my hotel. Her long black braid falls from a white fuzzy hat. She is young, vocal, and wears glasses. She takes me to Hippodrome Square next to the Blue Mosque. This is the ancient center of the city. Obelisks, including one from Roman times, pierce the sky. Romans held games and chariot races here. Another reminder of how old and layered Istanbul is. Some of the buildings that line the square display Eastern motifs, the first signs, Serap says, of the nationalistic architectural style that began to develop in Turkey at the turn of the century.

We walk in the sharp December cold to the Grand Bazaar. In the vaulted halls of the market armies of people stroll and shop for jewelry, brass, leather, carpets. We stop at the Oriental Cafe for *sahlep*, a drink of powdered orchid roots boiled in milk and sugar. "This is a famous old place," Serap says.

One of five children, Serap went to school in Ankara and did graduate work in Istanbul. She lives with her brother, a publisher, in a house that sometimes runs out of water. A few years ago, she was a fellow at the World Press Institute at Macalester College in St. Paul. Now she is an out of work journalist working parttime as a tour guide. She is applying for a job with Reuters. She hated her job writing for a weekly magazine and quit after five months. "I worked hard intellectually," she says. "I signed my name to articles about politics. The rest of the magazine was superficial. Lots of flashy photos."

Night is falling and with it rain as we enter the crowded food market. Shoppers snake through carts of chestnuts, pretzels, popcorn, *cay*, haggle over artful piles of nuts, dates, cheeses, mushrooms. The nose fills with smells, a rich fetid blend of earth, rain, spice, humanity. The market is noisy, chaotic, jostling, bristling with energy. Bare lightbulbs hang precariously above the stalls adding to the theatrical atmosphere. One fruitseller in heavy wool coat and cap beckons to us. He has a wonderfully craggy face with a thick black moustache and dark but tired eyes.

Previous pages: *Spices, Grand Bazaar*

Away from the market, we walk down a working class shopping street, also busy and colorful, the windows full of shoes, wedding gowns, giant loofahs, Christmas toys. Even in Islamic Turkey they recognize Christmas. People push through the street, arm in arm, talking, laughing, carrying bags full of things. Children run, dogs bark. Shoppers crowd in and out of the small brightly lit stores. There is a feeling, despite the rain and cold, of celebration in the air, of something vital and robust. One man carries on his back a basket full of beautiful yellow fruit topped with big dark green leaves.

We stop in the main post office, another early twentieth-century building. A large portrait of Atatürk, the father of modern Turkey, hangs on the wall. "He is my hero," Serap says. "He turned Turkey toward the West. We became a secular country and began using the Roman alphabet. He was very progressive, but he was an alcoholic. He died at fifty-six from cirrhosis of the liver."

We end up at the Galata Bridge, near the train station, "where the Orient Express stopped." We go to a small kebab place for dinner. A few men stare at a soccer match on a fuzzy television screen. There are no women. The food is simple, good, and cheap. Alcohol is not sold. "Can artists make a living in America?" Serap asks.

I ask Serap about the upcoming election. "Kurds are the main issue," she says. "I don't like the prime minister. She's conservative, I'm liberal." I tell her about the party I went to at the American Consulate. She tells me of past romances, including one with a Turkish man who went to the New School in New York and married someone else. "I hate love," she says with a smile. "I always fail. I am always so stupid when I am in love."

I walk back to the hotel in the rain. The Blue Mosque, lit behind webs of leafless branches, is preternaturally sublime. I fall asleep in my clothes to the sound of someone playing a piano. I wake up in the middle of the night disoriented, pick up my notebook, and write myself back to sleep.

ALONE BUT NOT LONELY

Today is another savagely cold day. It's not the best day for a boat ride, but the ferry is full nonetheless, with natives and a few tourists. The mosques of old Stamboul are shrouded in mist as the boat chugs away from the dock at the Galata Bridge. It is more fitting perhaps to see the domes and minarets this way, grayed and slightly phantasmagoric, than in bright sunlight. Just as it is to see the vast empty palaces and decaying *yalis* along the shores wrapped in the gloom of mystery. Istanbul is a city of interiors and secrets, of doors behind doors and slippery truths. It is a winter city, a city that, for all its physical pleasures, preys upon the mind, the imagination.

Other boats ply the strait — tankers, ferries, fishing trawls but no sailboats, not surprisingly. Red and white Turkish flags flap from masts and sterns, bursts of color in the blanket of gray. Gulls and cormorants dot the mournful sky. Along with the old *yalis* and palaces and mosques, many new buildings, residential and commercial, line the banks. Modern seething Istanbul sprawls and sprawls like every great city. We pass under long bridges including the graceful swan's neck of the Bosphorus Bridge.

Most passengers sit inside with a cup of Nescafé or a book or a child. Outside in the back of the ferry, a few of us brave the cold. The salt air, the icy waves of the Bosphorus, the droning ferry engine, the *yalis*, the mustachioed men I see through a porthole sipping tea, all of this, puts me squarely in another place, a different place. I am on a boat headed toward the Black Sea.

The boat crisscrosses back and forth across the water, stopping on the European side then on the Asian. The ferrymen tie up the boat at each village. Wet cigarettes hanging from their mouths, they skillfully wrap the big ropes around posts, unhook the chain to let people on and off all in a matter of minutes. At Sariyer, a fishing village at the top of the Bosphorus, the fish market is open and going strong. The fishmongers shriek into the cold air. Silver and white fish shine like strips of jewelry beneath the tarps.

I wander through the town in the rain then go into one of the fish restaurants that flank the market. I pick out a fish from a case in front of the restaurant. "Snapper," the waiter says. "Good." I am given a table on the third floor with a view through a lace curtain of the water. The only other customers are three Spaniards though when I leave two hours later the place is filled with locals.

The food is simply prepared, good if not great. The snapper is grilled and served whole, its tiny sharp teeth forming a sort of funny death smile. There is calamari, a green salad, a cooked apple-like fruit for dessert, Turkish white wine. The bow-tied waiter knows I am enjoying the meal, that I am content to be by myself. He is kind and polite. I linger with cups of Turkish coffee, writing, drawing, staring out at the bleak but somehow transfixing day. I would rather eat with my wife or friends, don't get me wrong, but solitude has its rewards. I have learned how to be self-contained, to be at ease with myself, to be, as A.J. Liebling said of his youthful days in Paris, alone but not lonely.

EVERY WHICH WAY

A courtyard outside the Eyup Mosque. Pigeons waddle across the heavy stones and perch in the giant plane trees. "Eyup was the disciple of the prophet Mohammed," Serap says. "His burial place is here. A kind of complex, or *külliye,* was built for him with a mosque and a mausoleum. It is the holiest place in Istanbul for Muslims. People everywhere make a pilgrimage to Eyup."

"Pigeons, too," I say as a mother and child crossing the courtyard spook hundreds of them. They turn this way then that in the sky, like a giant shaken rug, before lighting again.

"And storks," Serap says and points to one in a tree. "Storks that are hurt or lame are allowed to live here."

The *külliye* also included a market, a *caravanserai,* and a *hammam,* Serap tells me. Outside the mosque is a large wall of lovely old tiles arranged in a satisfyingly random way. Women in heavy winter coats and scarves pass by on their way to visit the holy *turbe.* We hike up a hill through a cemetery. Serap rubs her mittens together. It is bitterly cold again. The sky is Whistler gray. Across the hillside, among the weeds, grasses, dead flowers, and cypresses, are thousands of tombstones. They lean every which way, broken, crumbling, moss-covered. The organic chaos of graves and plants reminds me of the Jewish cemetery in Prague, but this place is much bigger and wilder. Even in winter you can see how overgrown the vegetation is. You can see how nature is allowed to have its way.

Most of the tombstones are narrow round columns or thin slabs with epitaphs in Turkish carved on the sides. A carved fez often sits on top of a man's stone, flowers on a woman's. "If the man was important," Serap says, "he might have a large turban on top." Other than some schoolboys scuffling along the path and a couple of men in heavy work clothes smoking cigarettes, there is no one around. Serap picks up a small stray kitten. "It must be freezing," she says.

Serap nuzzles the kitten as we walk along. The Golden Horn and Istanbul stretch

Pigeons, Eyup Mosque

into the distance. I have always been drawn to cemeteries. This one is not particularly haunting or melancholy, but there is something about its wildness that is striking. Turks must be on easier terms with death than Americans, more accepting of mortality. Most American cemeteries are neat and manicured. We try to control, to keep death at bay. Turks seem to yield to the chaos, to the inevitable.

"There aren't any weeds in our cemeteries," I say to Serap.

She puts the kitten in the pocket of her coat. "This place is eerie, don't you think?"

"It's beautiful."

GRACE

"I hope you will not be too bored," Tomur says as we take our seats. "There will be good drinks afterward." We are at the Ataturk Cultural Center for a ceremony honoring people in the arts, sciences, and sports. Tomur Atagök is an artist, a professor of art, and an elegant woman of a certain age.

I tell her I like her hat. "It's like a Turkish beret."

The awards are given annually by an association of newspapers. There is a minor scandal this year because no award is being given to a journalist. "The reporting was not good enough," Tomur says. "The newspapers are not critical enough of the government." After an intermission, a blond cabaret singer in a black dress with a split up the side belts out Turkish popular songs. She has a smoky voice. The crowd adores her.

"Why should you speak Turkish? Do you speak French?" Tomur asks me at the reception afterward. We are drinking *raki*. "Would you like some Turkish sweets?" She introduces me to the sculptor who won an award and to a scholar who was at the Institute for Oriental Studies at the University of Chicago for a number of years.

A woman complains of jet lag. "I just came back from the States," she says. "I gave a lecture at Harvard." Tomur explains that the woman is an art historian. "I was also in Washington. Have you seen the Vermeer exhibition?"

Tomur talks for a few minutes to several journalists, including a woman with curved painted nails and lipstick on her teeth who reminds me of Otto Dix's satirical portrait of a newspaperwoman. The scholar's wife, a dotty Englishwoman, a foot taller than her husband, looks around the crowded lobby. "Can you use your superior height to locate my little Turk?" she says to me. "We spend a lot of time away from each other. That's why we've been married for forty-five years."

Tomur and I retreat to the Marmara Hotel and sit in the bar overlooking Taksim Square. We order coffee, or rather Nescafé, and Tomur tells me about her life. During a long marriage to an American that ended in divorce, she lived at various times in Berkeley, Oklahoma, and South Carolina. "I liked the U.S.," she says. "I thought we would live there after my husband completed his Ph.D. here, but he liked Turkey too much. We never went back. He never finished his Ph.D." Their son is in Seattle working for Microsoft. "I am going to the U.S. soon. I have a Fulbright to organize a show of women artists from America and the Middle East."

Tomur's work is based on her diaries. She draws or paints and writes on small pieces of paper and puts them side by side, like pages. She frames every ten "pages" or so. "I started keeping a diary at night when I traveled alone in Europe. People really like this work."

It is easy to like Tomur. She is a worldly woman with a softness, an Eastern voluptuousness about her. Feminine, polite, and gifted in the art of conversation, she reminds me of Elisabeth Söderström and Josefina, the Argentine painter. "Tell me, David," Tomur asks, "what common themes have you found among the cities you've visited?"

I want to say something about the grace and gentility of women, but I don't.

EIGHT BELOW

At dinner in the hotel, I meet a Byzantine scholar from America. He is a small, polite, fastidious man. "I have been coming to Istanbul for thirty years," he says. "It has changed beyond belief. There used to be vast stretches of woods along the Bosphorus."

In the neighborhood around the Blue Mosque, neglected buildings lean into narrow streets, groups of men in smoke-filled cafés out of the rain play games with tiles, watch television, and drink tea. Windows of closed up shops are plastered with credit card decals. In one carpet store men sit in the dark rubbing their hands before a space heater. A big palace on one side of Hippodrome Square looks glamorous in the artificial light. Around the Hagia Sophia, people appear out of nowhere, as if from black pools of ether, a bit of legerdemain both enchanting and unsettling.

The cold bites but not as hard as the cold in Minnesota. "There's a blizzard," Wendy says over the phone. "It's eight degrees below zero, the wind chill is sixty below. The furnace is working fine. We'll survive."

TAKSIM SQUARE

Taksim Square may be the ugliest square I have seen. The center of modern European Istanbul is a circle of dirt, scrawny trees, and harried pedestrians, the depressing eye in a hurricane of traffic. Surrounding buildings — an old embassy, an old church, a bus station, and the modern glassy Ataturk Cultural Center, itself no beauty – are divorced from the square by the thundering traffic. Off to one side are statues of Ataturk and some of his fellow nationalists.

The square sits at the top of bustling Istiklal Caddesi, the old rue de Pera, downtown Istanbul's main street. The street teems with life much as it must have when the first foreign embassies went up along here hundreds of years ago. The only car is a streetcar. Past the old embassies are shops, cafés, movie houses, pretzel sellers, Christmas trees, strings of lights strung across turn-of-the-century apartment buildings. There is a steady flow in the cold gray afternoon of black-haired men and women in long coats, girls with back packs, and boys in blue blazers and ties, people shopping, eating kebabs, hanging out.

Small, melancholy courtyards with trellises of brown leaves open, like pockets, off side streets. Halfway down the street just off Galatasaray Square in an arcade is a market with stalls of gleaming fish and bright fruit, men in boots and aprons, smoking and drinking tea. Hungry cats and dogs, mill about, begging, scratching. One dog draws a bead on me and tags along, sniffing persistently as if it can't quite place the smell.

In an antique shop I find a book with photographs of Ottoman Istanbul, street scenes of extraordinary life and color, people in veils, baggy pants and turbans, men selling carpets, fish, spices. How will the pictures of our lives, our cities, look to the wandering souls of the future?

Along Istiklal Caddesi

A NIGHT WITH ORHAN

It is early evening in cold Istanbul. Orhan Taylan's studio, in the old Pera district, is up six flights of stairs. I am greeted by the smell of turpentine, the sound of jazz, and the painter, a small, graying man dressed in gray turtleneck and black jeans. The studio is large. Women are painting in several high-ceilinged rooms. One, who has red hair, he introduces as his assistant. There is a small kitchen and a view of the Bosphorus.

We sit down at a small table in the large foyer. Exhibition posters cover the front door. Numerous bookshelves cannot hold all the magazines and art books. Orhan pours two glasses of cold Dutch gin, lights my cigarette then his, and we begin to talk. We do not stop for seven hours. We talk about art, Istanbul, Europe, the U.S., language, politics, a lot about politics.

He tells me about his years in prison. "They gave electric shocks to my balls," he says. "They tortured us to try to get us to sign a statement denouncing the movement. No fucking way." An active leftist, he was part of the peace movement in the seventies opposed to Turkey's invasion of Cyprus. After the military coup in the early eighties, he and twenty or thirty others were rounded up.

"I was in military prisons first then civil prison. The guards and warden were more sympathetic in the civil prison. I was allowed to paint. I had an exhibition while I was in prison. Foreign diplomats and Turkish diplomats attended it. It was a kind of *cause célèbre*. I couldn't be there obviously. Amnesty International eventually got me released. The Dutch provided me with materials. One Dutchman drove from Holland with paints."

Now in his fifties, Orhan is a successful figurative painter. He recently bought a flat ten minutes away and converted it to a home and second studio. He also has a home on the sea in southern Turkey. To help pay the bills, he takes in students and mixes his own paints. "Imported paint is too expensive. We have good cheap linseed oil in Turkey. I am going to an opening tonight. Would you like to come?"

The exhibition is in the lobby of a bank. "Not great, are they?" Orhan says about the paintings. "She has sold a few. She is a friend, married to a rich textile man. They don't have good drinks. Let's get the hell out of here."

The Cinema Lovers Association is also known as Arif's Place. Arif, the owner, is a film producer who started the bar for movie people. It quickly became a hangout for artists and writers, for Istanbul's left-wing intelligentsia. It's a lively place. On the dark walls are posters of Marilyn Monroe and James Dean. We find a table and order *raki*.

People stop by the table to say hello – a woman sculptor and her husband, a well-known political columnist who smokes a pipe, a poet. The poet is in his cups. "He translates Russian poets into Turkish," Orhan says. "He is known more for this than for his poetry."

"Sad but true," the poet says.

"He is a wonderful poet. He was in prison with me," Orhan says and orders another round of *raki*. The ashtray fills up. The painter and the poet tell prison stories. They wear them like badges of honor. They talk about the need for intellectual freedom in Turkey.

"We must be able to talk openly without fear," the poet says.

"I am very pessimistic about Turkish politics," Orhan says. "The military is very strong. There is no leftist opposition. Young people who protest disappear. There is a mothers' vigil. Old people disappear, too. The state has all the power and control. Run by the elite for the rich. Nothing is done for the poor."

More people, mostly middle-aged with interesting faces, pile in. The bar gets smokier, noisier. We order more *raki*. Orhan is in high gear. "Inflation is our biggest problem. Over one hundred percent annually. Not to mention we are at war with the Kurds. Dozens of people die every day. It's guerilla warfare. The Kurds need autonomy, but the fundamentalists say no. They are fucking fascists. They are well organized and powerful. They are aided by the military. This is shit."

"How did you learn to swear so well in English?" I ask.

"I went to an American high-school in Istanbul. I can swear like a…a…."

"A sultan?"

"Like a sailor."

The night ends in a restaurant with a group of Americans and Turks, one of which is Orhan's estranged wife. We have to yell to be heard because everyone in the place is singing. A three-piece combo plays one mournful Turkish ballad after another and the well-dressed, professional-looking crowd sitting at long tables is shaking the rafters. They seem to know every word to every song. A few are dancing. The Turkish women at our table are dancing in their seats. When I ask the Turk next to me why he isn't singing along, he raises an eyebrow and blows smoke straight up.

Deafened by music, numbed by *raki*, Orhan and I say goodbye on Istiklal Cadessi. The boulevard is lined with metal trees with white lights. Taxis pull up, windows steamed in the cold. Clouds of exhaust and breath dot the air. Orhan's wife pushes him into one taxi, I scramble into another.

"You'll have to come back," Orhan says through the open window. "I don't think I'll ever make it to Minneapolis."

RUSSIAN NOVEL

The plane is over the Atlantic.

"Greenland is never green," the pilot says. Frozen white turf scrolls below my window. A plane zooms by, all metal and smoke, headed the other way, headed east. I thumb through my notebook. The year has been like a Russian novel, full of people and going on forever. I can still taste the raki from two nights ago. I think back to the first tentative days in Lima.

Clouds part. Minneapolis appears suddenly, a blanket of lights. "I see city," a child says. The wheels touch. A baby starts to cry.

"It's good to be back," the man next to me says.

I collect my bag and climb into a taxi.

It's snowing.

Home, Irving Avenue

MINNEAPOLIS

THE RIGHT ROOM

No full moon tonight, but snow is high in the yard and the wind when I turn the corner and head west makes me gasp. Rose, leash in her mouth, pulls me along. She is happy to be out of the house. The cold means nothing to her. I have walked these tree-lined streets, passed these gracious old houses a thousand times, but these days with the smell of India still in my nose, the blue of Iznik tiles in my eyes, my neighborhood seems the foreign place. It looks lovely in its winter whites, but the orderliness, sidewalks so neatly shoveled, and the serenity, living room lamps so diligently burning, and the prosperity, tend to rankle not comfort.

It's late, but I throw another log on the fire. Wendy, dozing in the big green chair, doesn't stir when we come in. A book sits precariously on her lap. Rose nudges her. Her eyes open briefly. "Did you have a nice walk?" She falls back asleep. Rose follows suit. She circles and paws her bed then flops with a contented sigh. I am too antsy to read. The voice on the radio tells me something by Schubert is coming up. I pour some whiskey and wait.

Not just for the music but for the feeling that comes over me late at night when the house is quiet. Around the room are paintings, shelves of books, family photographs, old furniture, patterned fabrics. My wife is folded like a child in the chair. With her thick curls and blissful look, she is a Pre-Raphaelite's dream.

The room, heavy with the history of my life, of my family's life, is sacred. At this moment, in the hushed night, I am content. The restlessness fades. Pascal was wrong. A man can sit quietly and happily in a room provided it's the right room. At least for awhile.

ACKNOWLEDGMENTS

I would like to thank St. Paul Companies (now St. Paul Travelers) for the generous grant that made my travels and this book possible. I am deeply grateful to Polly Nyberg whose support for the project, and for all my artistic endeavors, has been immeasurable. Many thanks to writers Judith Guest, Beth Dooley, and Jack El-Hai for their encouragement and advice. I am indebted to my son, David, who improved the manuscript considerably with his sharp pen and tactful suggestions. A great big thank-you goes to Kristen McDougall who designed the book. Without her, *The Nostalgic Heart* would not exist. Thanks very much to Lynn Oehler for her help with foreign languages and to Kevin Brown and Tim Kretzmann for technical assistance. To the many kind people around the world who welcomed me into their lives and cities, I extend my sincerest appreciation. Last of all, I want to thank Wendy, David, and Sarah. For their love and support, I count my blessings.

BIOGRAPHY

Photo: Gerald Gustafson

David Coggins is an artist, writer, and set designer. His paintings, drawings, and photographs have been exhibited in the U.S. and abroad. He has designed productions for theater and dance. *The Nostalgic Heart* is his first book.

Wall, Prague

Following pages:
Airport, Tokyo

ABOUT THE BOOK

Original images are photographs with mixed media (ink and paint).
Drawings are ink on paper.

The book was designed and composed by Kristen McDougall.
Typefaces are Griffo Classico (text) and Cochin (headings).
Griffo Classico is a revival design produced by Franko Luin in 1993.
It is based on types cut by Francesco Griffo for the Venetian printer
Aldus Manutius at the end of the fifteenth century.
Printed and bound by Friesens, Altona, Manitoba.

GATE	REMARKS		TIME	
			14:25	
C85	搭乗案内	NEW GATE	10:34	
E70	出発済み	DEPARTED	10:35	
C86	出発済み	DEPARTED	10:30	
C82	出発済み	DEPARTED		
E70	搭乗締切	GATE CLOSE		
B73	搭乗中	BOARDING		
E70	搭乗中	BOARDING		
A63	搭乗中	BOARDING		
C83	搭乗中	BOARDING		
D91	出国手続中	CLEARING		
C88	出国手続中	CLEARING		
C87	出国手続中	CLEARING		
D93	出国手続中	CLEARING		
D95	出国手続中	CLEARING		
D95	出国手続中	CLEARING		
A62	出国手続中	CLEARING		
70	出国手続中	CLEARING		
70	出国手続中	CLEARING		
74	出国手続中	CLEARING		
85	出国手続中	CLEARING		
1	出国手続中	CLEARING		
2	出国手続中	CLEARING		
	出国手続中	CLEARING		
2	出国手続中	CLEARING		

TIME	
12:30	AMST
12:35	
12:45	
13:00	MOSC
13:00	MANI
13:00	MOSC
13:10	
13:30	
13:35	SHAN
14:00	
14:55	
14:55	CEBU
15:50	
15:55	SHAN
16:00	MANI
16:20	
16:55	
17:00	TAIP
17:20	
17:30	
17:40	
18:00	
18:30	
18:30	

TO	AIRLINE	FLIGHT NO.	GATE
	JAL	JL411	D94
ZURICH	SAS	SK984	D96
COPENHAGEN	SAS	SK984	D96
ZURICH	SWISSAIR	SR169	C81
MADRID	IBERIA	IB6710	C84
KARACHI	PIA	PK9761	B73
PARIS	AEROFLOT	SU576	C86
KUALA LUMPUR	JAL	JL723	C82
SEOUL	ASIANA	OZ101	D91
BEIJING	CHINAEASTERN	MU524	C88
FRANKFURT	JAL	JL407	C83
BEIJING	AIR CHINA	CA926	D96
MANILA	PHILIPPINES	PR433	C86
SINGAPORE	ANA	NH901	
BEIJING	AIR CHINA	CA920	C84
CAIRO	EGYPT AIR	MS865	B7
BANGKOK	ANA	NH915	
HONG KONG	JAL	JL1	D9
PHUKET	THAI	TG671	D9
LOS ANGELES	JAL	JL62	D9
SINGAPORE	JAL	JL711	C
LOS ANGELES	ANA	NH6	
SAN FRANCISCO	JAL	JL2	C
KANSAI	JAL	JL51	
HONG KONG	JAL	JL735